CYCLING
SOUTH
LEINSTER

y & A : Service

GREAT ROAD ROUTES

TURLOUGH O'BRIEN, from Carlow, is CEO of Carlow Voluntary Housing Association and manager of the Carlow Senior Football Team. He developed a love of cycling as a teenager and has cycled extensively in Ireland, England, France, Switzerland, Italy and USA. With a deep interest in ancient pilgrimage routes, he has cycled the Via Francigena from Canterbury to Rome, as well as cycling the Camino de Santiago on many occasions.

Stay up to date with the author at:

 @TurloughCarlow

 www.rotharroutes.com

Downhill to Old Leighlin, County Carlow

Advice to Readers

Every effort is made by our authors to ensure the accuracy of our guidebooks. However, changes can occur after a book has been printed. If you notice discrepancies between this guidebook and the facts on the ground, please let us know, either by email to enquiries@collinspress.ie or by post to The Collins Press, West Link Park, Doughcloyne, Wilton, Cork, T12 N5EF, Ireland.

Crossing the bridge over the River Nore at Inistioge in County Kilkenny

CYCLING
SOUTH
LEINSTER
GREAT ROAD ROUTES

TURLOUGH O'BRIEN

The Collins Press

To my wife, Mary and our sons Cian, Darragh and Ronan

FIRST PUBLISHED IN 2017 BY
The Collins Press
West Link Park
Doughcloyne
Wilton
Cork
T12 N5EF
Ireland

A CIP record for this book is available from the British Library.

Paperback ISBN: 978-1-84889-305-4

Design and typesetting by Fairways Design
Typeset in Myriad Pro
Printed in Poland by Białostockie Zakłady Graficzne SA

Contents

Acknowledgements   7

Map of Route Start Points   8

Quick-Reference Route Table   10

Introduction   13

How To Use This Book   15

Routes

1. The Curragh of Kildare   20

2. Timahoe Loop   24

3. Castledermot Circuit   28

4. The Hidden Sky Road   32

5. To Arthur's Way and Beyond!   35

6. Barrow to The Nore Loop   40

7. Bilboa and Back   44

8. Ring of Hook Bike Route   48

9. Durrow Loop   52

10. East Carlow Circuit   56

11. Johnstown Castle Ring   60

12. Sallins Loop   63

13. The Bog of Allen Circuit   68

14. Vicarstown/Emo Circuit   72

15. Carlow Town Loop   76

16. Abbeyleix and Wolfhill Route   80

17. Ballitore/Glen of Imaal Circuit   84

18. On the Trail of the Saints   88

19. Rebel River Route   93

20. Lap of the Lakes   97

21. Dunbrody Trail   101

22. Bagenalstown/Drumphea Route 105

23. Paulstown Route 110

24. Tour of the Blackstairs 114

25. Inistioge Route 119

26. North Kilkenny Cycle Route 124

27. The Three Sisters Tour 128

28. Ollie Walsh Way 132

29. Slieve Blooms – The Three Peaks Challenge 136

30. Follow Me Up to Carlow 140

Acknowledgements

A task such as this could not have been completed without the help, advice and support of many.

The seed was sown by Dermot Mulligan, curator of the wonderful Carlow Museum; but for his encouragement the opportunity would have passed me by.

Behind every good man is a good woman and my wife, Mary, was not only as supportive as ever but was also my cycling partner on many of the routes. In the earlier routes she really tested my levels of fitness as she chatted freely while I could hardly draw breath!

My sons Cian, Darragh and Ronan goaded, prodded and cajoled me in equal measure to keep going and to focus on completing the book, one route at a time.

Thanks to my brother Dermot and old friend John Owens for cycling some of the routes; it was so much easier with company.

Map of Route Start Points

1. The Curragh of Kildare

2. Timahoe Loop

3. Castledermot Circuit

4. The Hidden Sky Road

5. To Arthur's Way and Beyond!

6. Barrow to the Nore Loop

7. Bilboa and Back

8. Ring of Hook Bike Route

9. Durrow Loop

10. East Carlow Circuit

11. Johnstown Castle Ring

12. Sallins Loop

13. The Bog of Allen Circuit

14. Vicarstown/Emo Circuit

15. Carlow Town Loop

16. Abbeyleix and Wolfhill Route

17. Ballitore/Glen of Imaal Circuit

18. On the Trail of the Saints

19. Rebel River Route

20. Lap of the Lakes

21. Dunbrody Trail

22. Bagenalstown/Drumphea Route

23. Paulstown Route

24. Tour of the Blackstairs

25. Inistioge Route

26. North Kilkenny Cycle Route

27. The Three Sisters Tour

28. Ollie Walsh Way

29. Slieve Blooms – Three Peaks Challenge

30. Follow Me Up to Carlow

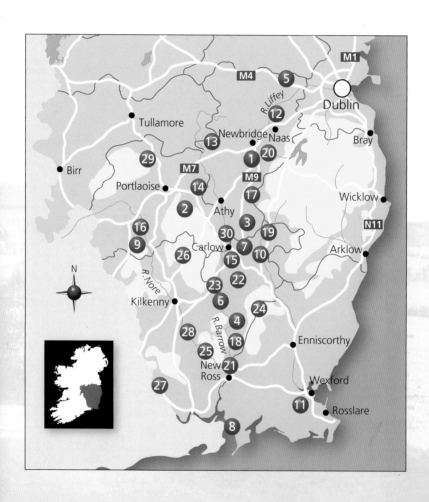

M1

M4

5

R.Liffey

12

Dublin

Tullamore

13

Newbridge Naas

20

Bray

29

1

Birr

M7

14

Portlaoise

M9

17

Wicklow

2

Athy

N11

16

3

19

9

30

7

Carlow

10

Arklow

26

15

22

23

6

Kilkenny

24

R.Nore

N

28

R.Barrow

4

18

Enniscorthy

25

21

New Ross

Wexford

27

11

8

Rosslare

9

Quick-Reference Route Table

No.	County	Route	Grade	Range
1	Kildare	The Curragh of Kildare	1	Short
2	Laois	Timahoe Loop	2	Short
3	Kildare	Castledermot Circuit	2	Short
4	Carlow	The Hidden Sky Road	3	Short
5	Kildare	To Arthur's Way and Beyond!	2	Mid
6	Kilkenny	Barrow to the Nore Loop	3	Mid
7	Carlow/Laois	Bilboa and Back	3	Mid
8	Wexford	Ring of Hook Bike Route	2	Mid
9	Laois/Kilkenny	Durrow Loop	2	Mid
10	Carlow	East Carlow Circuit	4	Mid
11	Wexford	Johnstown Castle Ring	2	Mid
12	Kildare	Sallins Loop	2	Mid
13	Kildare/Offaly	The Bog of Allen Circuit	2	Mid
14	Laois/Kildare	Vicarstown/Emo Circuit	2	Mid
15	Carlow/ Laois/Kildare	Carlow Town Loop	3	Mid
16	Laois/Kilkenny	Abbeyleix and Wolfhill Route	3	Mid
17	Kildare/Wicklow	Ballitore/Glen of Imaal Circuit	3	Mid
18	Carlow/Wexford/Kilkenny	On the Trail of the Saints	4	Mid
19	Carlow/Wicklow	Rebel River Route	4	Mid
20	Kildare/Wicklow	Lap of the Lakes	3	Mid
21	Wexford/Waterford	Dunbrody Trail	3	Mid
22	Carlow	Bagenalstown/Drumphea Route	3	Mid
23	Kilkenny	Paulstown Route	3	Long
24	Carlow	Tour of the Blackstairs	4	Long
25	Kilkenny	Inistioge Route	5	Long
26	Kilkenny	North Kilkenny Cycle Route	4	Long
27	Kilkenny	The Three Sisters Tour	5	Long
28	Kilkenny	Ollie Walsh Way	5	Long
29	Laois/Offaly	Slieve Blooms – Three Peaks Challenge	5	Long
30	Carlow	Follow Me Up to Carlow	5	Long

Distance	Ascent	Time	Category	Page
27	160	1½ hours	Flat	20
35	334	1½–2 hours	Rolling	24
36	311	1½–2 hours	Rolling	28
36	473	2 hours	Hilly	32
41	219	1½–2 hours	Flat	35
42	442	2–2½ hours	Hilly	40
44	519	2½–3 hours	Hilly	44
44	326	2–3 hours	Flat	48
45	501	2–2½ hours	Hilly	52
52	611	2½–3 hours	Hilly	56
54	289	2–2½ hours	Flat	60
55	256	2½–3 hours	Flat	63
56	230	2½–3 hours	Flat	68
56	327	2½–3 hours	Flat–Rolling	72
58	466	2½–3 hours	Flat–Hilly	76
58	517	2½–3 hours	Hilly	80
59	618	3–3½ hours	Hilly	84
61	817	3–3½ hours	Hilly	88
64	678	3–3½ hours	Hilly	93
67	638	3–3½ hours	Hilly	97
67	987	3¾–4¼ hours	Flat–Mountainous	101
69	652	3–3½ hours	Flat–Hilly	105
72	584	3¼–3¾ hours	Hilly	110
76	1,028	4–4½ hours	Mountainous	114
80	1,203	4½–5 hours	Mountainous	119
81	855	4–4½ hours	Hilly	124
88	1,004	4–4½ hours	Mountainous	128
90	974	4½–5 hours	Mountainous	132
92	1,363	5–5½ hours	Mountainous	136
103	704	4½–5½ hours	Hilly	140

Cúl na Sneachta and beyond,
Mount Leinster, County Carlow

Introduction

My interest in cycling grew out of my family's involvement in the GAA. My father, Jim, was County Secretary when I was a young teenager. During the summer holidays I was enlisted to deliver the post by bicycle to all the club secretaries across County Carlow. I quickly got to know the beautiful townland names and the shortest routes along the back roads of the county. And it went from there!

For years I've been cycling the back roads of south Leinster and working out the best routes to open up this unspoilt landscape for fellow cyclists and visitors. The biggest difficulty has been deciding what to omit: there is unbelievable variety in the south-east, serviced by a terrific network of local roads – over 14,000km of roads in Counties Carlow, Kilkenny, Laois, Kildare, Wicklow and Wexford. This guide covers just short of 2,000km and involves almost 20,000 metres of climbing!

Whether you like the challenging gradients of the mountains or freewheeling in the flatlands, this guide has you covered. No matter which route you ride, you are sure of a memorable cycle.

Ernest Hemingway said, 'It is by riding a bicycle that you learn the contours of a country best, since you have to sweat up the hills and coast down them. Thus you remember them as they actually are, while in a motor car only a high hill impresses you, and you have no such accurate remembrance of country you have driven through as you gain by riding a bicycle.'

As I meandered along the boreens of Kilkenny in particular, his words rang true. Kilkenny is far from flat, as you will discover!

Cycling heightens the senses. One of the many joys of cruising along the back roads on your bike is hearing songbirds in the hedgerows and trying to identify which birds you hear. And the sense of smell is stimulated with the earthiness of freshly ploughed fields, the musky scent of fields of rapeseed or the smell of freshly cut silage.

I have been amazed, as Mike Carter observed in his 2011 book *One Man and His Bike*, published by Ebury Press, at 'how much I could tell about a vehicle approaching from behind: how big it was; how quickly it was traveling; how aggressively it was being driven, even … being able to extrapolate, from all that noise, how much room it was likely to give me while passing'.

The network of back roads is one of our great cycling assets, particularly valued by urban dwellers. It allows the mind and body to relax and enjoy hassle-free cycling for mile after glorious mile. Nothing beats the feeling of effortlessly ghosting along on these quiet roads with a wind at your back.

There is a great sense of a true journey, where every turn in the road, every hill climbed becomes a milestone, a feeling that can never be obtained travelling by car.

I loved every aspect of writing this guidebook: researching routes and local history, identifying places of interest that are off the beaten track; then cycling the routes, mapping and photographing them and writing descriptions. I have aimed to provide you with ready-made routes that will provide you with hours of fantastic cycling in one of the world's best cycling environments and all in stunning locations.

These hidden gems are unlocked by the marvellous network of local roads across the region; with this guidebook in your backpack all you have to do is get out there and enjoy the beauty of south Leinster.

The routes are circuits to allow you start and finish at the same place, and are of varying distances. Many of the routes intersect to form a necklace of routes, allowing you to combine routes if you desire to extend your cycling.

South Leinster is part of Ireland's Ancient East and the region is abundant in heritage sites. There are so many points of interest on all routes, it is like travelling in a time machine as you are transported through the ages.

I wish you a fair wind for your cycling across south Leinster!

How to use this book

At the beginning of each route is some key information of the route characteristics: the location, grade, distance covered, the height gain of the route, duration and my verdict of the route. There is also a ribbon listing the towns and villages visited. For example:

Bagenalstown

Bagenalstown – Ballinkillen – Drumphea – Altamont Gardens – The Fighting Cocks – Bagenalstown

Location	County Carlow
Grade	3
Distance	69km
Height gain	652 metres
Duration	3–3½ hours
Verdict	Unspoilt rural route on country roads with great views across County Carlow

Grading

The routes are graded as follows:

Grade

1 The easiest routes; very short – less than 30km, little climbing.

2 Distances can be up to 60km, rolling hills.

3 Hilly routes that combine with long flat sections.

4 Steep climbs over short distances interspersed with less challenging sections.

5 Challenging routes, combining longer distances and or extensive climbing.

Gradings are subjective but are consistently applied. The shorter the distance, generally the easier the cycle. I have factored in the amount of climbing and the recovery between climbs, which is indicated on the elevation charts supplied.

Obviously, inexperienced cyclists should begin with the shorter distances and not be too ambitious, especially in tackling hilly routes.

The routes utilise the local and regional road network as much as possible. I have tried to stay off national routes, indeed sometimes the routes are extended to avoid busy sections of national routes.

Because many of the routes follow local roads in remote areas it is best to have a cycling partner along in case of mechanical problems or accidents. At the very least, always let someone know where you are cycling and at what time you expect to return.

Principal road numbers are shown on the maps. I recommend bringing the appropriate OS *Discovery* maps, which can provide greater detail than the illustrative maps here in the guide.

Comfort and Safety

The number one thing that turns many a novice cyclist off cycling is … a sore bum! Wearing padded shorts is essential when cycling for any significant distance.

A comfortable saddle that is a good fit will also help.

You don't have to be dressed like a competitor in the Tour de France but I do recommend wearing bright clothing on a bike. Being visible is vital, especially when weather conditions deteriorate or light fades. There are lots of cheap and sensible options available now to ensure you are kept both warm and visible.

I recommend layers; you can put them on or take them off as conditions dictate.

Don't leave home without a helmet. All cyclists experience a fall at some stage and a helmet can be life saving.

Cycling gloves do more than keep your hands warm: they are padded to reduce friction between your palms and the handlebars, dampen vibrations and prevent numbness. They are also used to wipe sweat away from your brow and are very handy if you are unfortunate enough to have a tumble!

Good footwear is as important when cycling as when walking or running. Many cyclists use dedicated cycling shoes and use clip-less pedals which attach them to the bike. These assist in a more efficient cycling technique, which is very beneficial on longer routes. At the very least, I recommend a runner with a hard sole for comfort.

There are all kinds of lighting options nowadays. Most lights are removable to prevent theft and you should always bring lights with you; it's not worth getting caught out because a cycle took longer than anticipated or light conditions deteriorated.

It should really go without saying, but I will, anyway: obey the rules of the road. Keep well to the left but be careful because of drains, potholes and debris. If cycling as part of a group, two abreast is recommended but not when overtaking. Use clear hand signals when turning and approaching roundabouts while being careful to keep control of the bike.

A rear-view mirror is a useful addition. These can be handlebar- or helmet-mounted.

A set of panniers or a small backpack are very useful for carrying snacks and fluids, additional clothing – the weather can change suddenly and there is nothing worse than a drenching on a long-distance cycle – and possibly a camera.

It's all about the bike

There have been spectacular advancements in bicycle technology and design; there are purpose-built bikes to choose from – racing, mountain, commuter, hybrid and even recumbent bicycles. Don't feel it is necessary to spend a fortune to acquire a bike capable of completing the routes in this book. The first time I cycled the Camino in Spain I did it on a town bike!

There are a few essential requirements to ensure cycling is safe, comfortable and efficient. Make sure you have the right size of bike: frames come in different sizes and it isn't a case that one size fits all. Make sure to get this basic right, regardless of the type of bike you use.

Most modern bikes come with plenty of gears. This is important as you will be cycling on a lot of hilly routes and you need to be able to select the gear that allows you to pedal at a comfortable rate. The gear you use is down to personal preference and you will want to be able to select a gear to suit the terrain and weather conditions; cycling into a wind requires much more effort than having a tailwind. Good gear selection reduces the effort required to maintain a comfortable cadence.

All these routes can be completed on almost any type of bike – as long as the bike is well maintained. Have it serviced regularly.

Equally important is to give a pre-check before you leave the house.

- Check your tyres for wear and tear, and check the air pressure. Proper air pressure is really important; under-inflated tyres create a drag and slow you down – and are more likely to puncture.
- Inspect your brakes – really important on these hilly routes! Worn brake pads should be replaced; you are playing Russian roulette on wheels if you are not inspecting them.
- The chain should be oiled and lubricated (lightly). Ensure the gears are not slipping and that gear shifting is smooth.
- Check pannier racks are secure and that nuts are tightened.
- Make sure you have a good pump, spare tubes, a puncture-repair kit, tyre levers and a multitool in case of emergencies.

Useful websites

My website, www.rotharroutes.come has lots of information on cycling at home and abroad.

Tourism
http://carlowtourism.com
www.kildare.ie/tourism/
www.southlaoistourism.com/activities/cycle-trails/
http://visitkilkenny.ie/kilkenny_trails

www.visitwexford.ie
http://visitwicklow.ie

Heritage
www.heritageireland.ie/en/south-east/
www.megalithomania.com

Transport
www.buseireann.ie
www.irishrail.ie
www.jjkavanagh.ie

Cycling
www.connect.garmin.com
www.cyclingireland.ie
www.cyclinguk.org
https://cyclist.ie
www.irishcycling.com
www.ridewithgps.com

Climate

Ireland's temperate climate and prevailing south-westerly winds mean unpredictable weather. Our warmest months are also our wettest. However, south Leinster is Ireland's sunniest region. Keep an eye on the weather forecast and bring adequate clothing. An easily folded rain cape is always a good option, just in case. How many layers of clothing you should wear depends on personal preference but warm clothing can be advisable for many cycles in spring, autumn and winter.

Contacts

Emergency Services: For all emergencies dial 999. This includes the Garda Síochána, ambulance, fire brigade, mountain rescue and coastguard. You can also dial the EU number 112, which connects to the same services. Both numbers are free of charge.

Weather Forecast: For weather forecasts check the Met Éireann website (www.met.ie) or www.mountain-forecast.com. The accuweather.com app also has good information.

Map Information

Map information from this book was based on GPS and maps generated using ridewithgps.com and Garmin Edge Touring GPS Cycle Computer.

Leafy canopy at Tuckmill, Baltinglass, County Wicklow

1. The Curragh of Kildare

Athgarvan Heights – Brownstown – Irish National Stud – Kildare –
Little Curragh – Pollardstown Fen – The Curragh Racecourse –
Dan Donnelly's Hollow – Athgarvan Heights

Location: County Kildare	**Grade:** 1
Distance: 27km	**Height Gain:** 160 metres
Duration: 1½ hours	

Verdict: Unique plains setting better known for horses, sheep and Army HQ!

Start/Finish

You can pick almost anywhere to start this short and unique cycle route. If approaching on the M7 from Dublin, exit at Junction 12. Turn left onto the R413 as far as Donnelly's Hollow. Turn right onto the L7034, pass through Royal Curragh Golf Club and turn left up a short hill. The top of the hill is a popular parking spot for walkers on the Curragh Plains.

Round tower in Kildare town, County Kildare

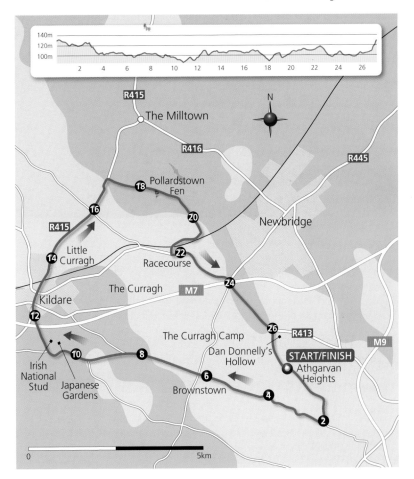

Route Highlights

This may be the shortest route in this guide but it is set in a unique Irish landscape worth an in-depth visit. The road skirts the boundary of the famed open plain, often called Saint Brigid's Pastures. The flat pasture of nearly 5,000 acres still retains the right of commonage for grazing sheep, which supposedly originated with the saint. Around its edges are some important attractions, which merit a visit.

Route Description

As the Curragh is so exposed, it is advisable to check the wind direction before starting out; my preference is to cycle into the wind on the outward journey and return with the wind at my back!

21

Dan Donnelly's Hollow in the Curragh, County Kildare

It is an easy route to navigate; I travelled clockwise and followed the perimeter of the Curragh. Park the car at Athgarvan Heights and follow the road in an easterly direction along the edge of the plain. Watch out for the sheep! The Curragh will be on your right-hand side all the way around.

The low hills of the early section are covered in colourful gorse. After 2km turn right at a T-junction and continue straight ahead. The army firing ranges are located in this area, as is 'Braveheart Hill', used in a scene from the film *Braveheart*, which starred Mel Gibson.

At 4km from the T-junction you meet a busy intersection where traffic from the Curragh Camp crosses towards Suncroft at Brownstown. Continue straight ahead until you meet a fork in the road. Take the left fork, which will bring you towards the Irish National Stud, The Japanese Gardens and St Fiachra's Garden. These are popular tourist attractions in County Kildare and it is worth stopping to explore their beauty.

The Japanese Gardens are the finest in Europe and are a feast for the senses. St Fiachra's Garden is a relative newcomer, designed only in 1999 to commemorate the Irish monastic movement and named after the patron saint of gardening himself, St Fiachra. Nothing epitomises Kildare more than the thoroughbred industry. The National Stud is a thoroughbred horse-breeding facility and is home to some of the most magnificent stallions that spend their retirement years here. It's a day out in itself!

Our journey continues past the gardens, crosses over the M7 and soon you arrive into Kildare town. There are plenty of gastro pubs and cafes close by the cathedral and round tower. Kildare is closely associated with St Brigid and the cathedral and round tower are named after the patron saint of the diocese.

The entrance to the round tower is located in the main square in the town. After you visit it, turn left when exiting onto the R415. Stay on this road which crosses the Little Curragh before taking a right turn after 4km signposted to Pollardstown Fen which is 3km ahead on the left-hand side.

The Fen is a rare ecosystem in Ireland and indeed Europe. It's well worth rambling through, for nature lovers, which most touring cyclists tend to be.

Continue past the Fen and after 1.2km make a right-hand turn, signposted for Moorefield GAA.

Stay on the road until the Curragh comes into view again and turn left onto the R413. The road curves around the grandstand of the racecourse and continues to a very busy roundabout. Take the third exit off the roundabout and continue to the second roundabout, where you take the first exit. Take care as you traverse this busy intersection. You are now at the point where you drove onto the Curragh.

Follow the route ahead but make sure to visit Donnelly's Hollow which is just beyond the right-hand turn you used when you drove in.

Dan Donnelly was a famous Irish boxer in the early 1800s who fought many a prize fight in the famed hollow, attracting huge crowds. As famous as he was when alive he achieved even more fame after he died when his body was stolen by medical students. The body was purchased from them by the eminent Dublin surgeon Hall who removed the right arm to study the muscle structure and respectfully buried the body. The arm was eventually purchased by a travelling circus, which exhibited it during shows. It later was acquired by Hugh 'Texas' McAlevey, a wealthy Ulster bookmaker. Eventually Dan Donnelly's right arm found a home in The Hideout pub in Kilcullen.

Well worth a look and you can imagine the scene of the packed hollow as the fights took place!

Leave the hollow and turn left to return to the car.

Curragh Race Track, County Kildare

2. Timahoe Loop

Timahoe – The Windy Gap – Stradbally – Rock of Dunamase – Timahoe

Location: County Laois

Distance: 35km

Duration: 1½–2 hours

Grade: 2

Height Gain: 334 metres

Verdict: Picturesque short route

Start/Finish

Timahoe is about 12km south of Portlaoise and 9km west of Stradbally. Park near the round tower.

Route Highlights

The route is steeped in history and there are stunning views of rolling woodland, hilltops covered in mighty oak and horse chestnut trees, brilliant green pastures interspersed with fields of golden barley and wheat, a veritable feast for the eye.

Rock of Dunamase, County Laois

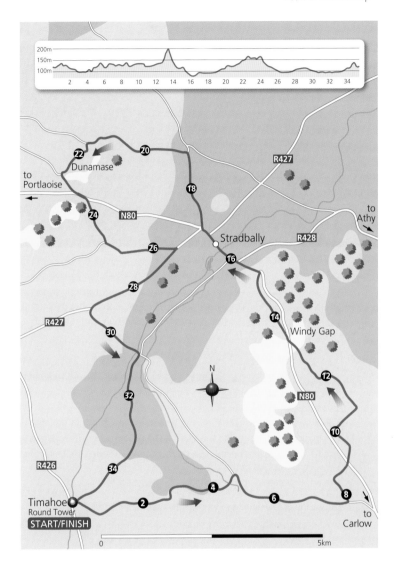

Route Description

The pretty, sleepy village of Timahoe with its village green is off the beaten track but is well known as the location of one of Ireland's finest round towers, standing 30 metres high and featuring a stunning Romanesque doorway. It's a great sight as you approach the village, especially across the hill from the neighbouring village of The Swan.

The Windy Gap, County Laois

The roads around here are quiet and ideal for cycling. With the round tower at your back, cycle clockwise around the green and turn right in 100 metres onto the L3840, signposted towards Luggacurren. Continue on this windy road for just over 4km, pass over a stone bridge over the Crooked River and turn right at the T-junction. Stay on this road for 3km and then, just over the brow of a small hill, take the left-hand turn onto a narrow road; continue to a T-junction, go right and shortly cross the busy N80. You could take the N80 but far better to stick with the byroads and enjoy a peaceful cycle devoid of traffic.

Having crossed over, follow the road as it veers left parallel to the N80 until a T-junction. Turn right, and then left at the next crossroads. You face a short, stiff climb with a minimum 8% gradient but the pain is short-lived! The road rejoins the N80 at the top of the Windy Gap where the views in front are simply breathtaking and among the finest pastoral landscapes in the country.

You have the option of cycling on the N80 into Stradbally or, if on a hybrid, touring or mountain bike, there is a laneway on the opposite side that will bring you nicely down towards the *Sráid Bhaile*, as Stradbally is called in Irish, after it merges with the N80 just below the graveyard.

Stradbally is possibly better known today thanks to the Electric Picnic, a music and arts festival that is held on the grounds of Stradbally Hall, but it is equally well known for the steam rally (held annually at the start of August) and the aforementioned Stradbally Hall, ancestral home of the Cosbys. It's a great stopping-off point for a cup of coffee or a snack.

Resume your cycle by continuing up the main street and taking the right-hand turn at the top of the hill in the direction of The Heath. Take the next left turn after about 1.5km and continue on this gently rising road until it brings you around to a view of the famed Rock of Dunamase.

This hilltop fortress, former home of the O'Moores of Laois, is an impressive heritage site worth exploring on foot. Park up and stroll through the labyrinth of ruins and admire the views from this rocky perch. Retrace your footsteps back to your trusty steed and head for Stradbally, taking the right-hand fork where it meets the road you travelled here on. The road comes out onto the very busy main road at quite a dangerous junction. Turn left with care onto the main road but travelling downhill you quickly exit onto a minor road on the right-hand side after just 200 metres. Stay on this road for about 3km until it meets the R427.

Turn right onto the R427 at the rear entrance to the Stradbally Estate. Cycle west in the direction of the signposted Ballyroan and Abbeyleix, alongside the wooded boundary of Stradbally Estate for 2.5km. Take the first left turn onto the L7834, followed shortly by another left. The roads here traverse a flat plain with fine views of the surrounding hilltops. In 1.5km pass over an old stone bridge and turn right. Continue for just over 4km to return to Timahoe.

View from the Rock of Dunamase, County Laois

3. Castledermot Circuit

Castledermot – Kilkea – Moone High Cross Inn – Moone – Ballitore – Frocken Hill – Castledermot

Location: County Kildare

Distance: 36km

Duration: 1½–2 hours

Verdict: Quiet roads for contemplation!

Grade: 2

Height Gain: 311 metres

Cycling around historic Kilkea Castle

Start/Finish

Castledermot is a historic village in south Kildare easily accessed from the M9. Take exit 4 onto the R448 and follow the signs to Castledermot which is just 2km away. On-street parking is available in the village. Use Castledermot Abbey, on the main street, as your starting point.

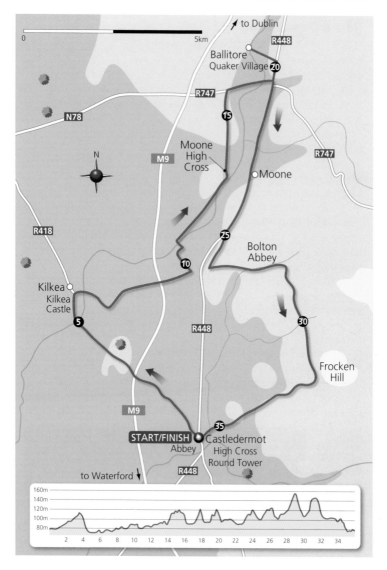

Route Highlights

A very pleasant and interesting loop on good roads with little traffic and lots of interesting sights. Kilkea Castle has a long history and the village is the birthplace of Antarctic explorer Ernest Shackleton. Moone High Cross is one of the best examples in the country and well worth investigating.

Route Description

Start this refreshing cycle from Castledermot Abbey. The key to the gate can be obtained in the house on the left-hand side. The ruins are hugely impressive from the inside and worth viewing.

Again before leaving, cross the main street and head into the grounds of St James' Church of Ireland where you will find two fine examples of Irish high crosses, a round tower and a unique hogback stone, evidence of the presence of Vikings in the area. This was the important monastic site of Diseart Diarmada.

Return to the main street and turn right towards the traffic lights; turn left at the lights and you will find yourself on a really good cycling road which will take you to beautiful Kilkea, 6km distant.

Kilkea Castle is a stunning twelfth-century castle, home of the Fitzgeralds, Earls of Kildare. The castle was a top-class hotel and golf resort for many years, but unfortunately fell victim to the economic downturn post-Celtic Tiger and is no longer open, though at the time of writing it had recently been sold. It has an enchanting history – associated with 'The Wizard Earl' who practised alchemy and was reputed to have magic powers. They say the castle is haunted and that he returns every seven years on a white horse!

The Antarctic explorer Ernest Shackleton was born here in Kilkea and a statue has recently been erected in nearby Athy in his honour. There's a fine Shackleton museum in the Athy Heritage Centre.

Take the narrow road leading away to the left of the main gates and continue around the edge of the estate to the T-junction and go left. These are quiet roads among lush green pastures and make for very pleasant cycling. Continue straight ahead for approximately 3km until the next

Moone High Cross Inn, County Kildare

T-junction. The Moone High Cross Inn is on your right and is worthy of a stop as the owner has a great collection of farm implements and curiosities. Refreshments are available.

Retrace your steps and continue straight ahead. Take the next right-hand turn, just after the bridge over the River Griese on a small hill and continue onwards with the small river over your right shoulder. Turn left at the next T-junction and be sure to stop and visit Moone High Cross. This is one of the finest high crosses in the country.

Turn right when leaving the high cross and stay on this quiet road until it meets up with the R747, turn right onto it and then left on the R448 staying on it for 2km approximately. A left turn will take you to the Quaker village of Ballitore.

In 1685 two Quakers decided to settle beside the River Griese, and the story of Ballitore began. They built woollen and flour mills, and over the next two centuries more Quakers settled and developed what became known as the Quaker village. In 1726 Abraham Shackleton started the famous Ballitore boarding school

Moone High Cross, County Kildare

which lasted for over a century and numbered Edmund Burke, Paul (later Cardinal) Cullen and Napper Tandy among its pupils. In the last century the village went into decline, but twenty years ago saw the start of its revival, and now it is once again attractive, with the old Meeting House refurbished and Mary Leadbeater's house rebuilt and housing the library and a small Quaker museum. The museum is open during the week, and also on Sundays from June to September between 2 p.m. and 6 p.m.

Return to the R448 and turn back, to the right, staying on this wide, well-surfaced road for 5km approximately. Turn left onto a small side road that continues uphill. At the top of the hill take a left-hand turn which will take you past Bolton Abbey and its community of Cistercian monks.

Take the next left, followed by two right-hand turns and continue on this undulating road for 4km to a crossroads on the side of Frocken Hill. Take the right-hand turn and stay on the road, which will lead you back to Castledermot in 4km. A lovely spin on a summer evening!

31

4. The Hidden Sky Road

Borris – Slievebawn – Cúl na Sneachta – Myshall – Garryhill – Borris

Location: County Carlow

Distance: 36km

Duration: 2 hours

Verdict: Great short cycle featuring good climbing and views

Grade: 3

Height Gain: 473 metres

Start/Finish

Borris is situated 30km south of Carlow and 26km east of Kilkenny. Coming from Carlow, take exit 6 off the M9 and continue through Leighlinbridge and Bagenalstown. If coming from Kilkenny, take exit 7 at Paulstown and continue through Goresbridge to Borris. Park on the main street.

Route Highlights

A short but surprisingly interesting loop on some of the most scenic roads in the south-east.

Adelaide Memorial Church in Myshall, County Carlow.

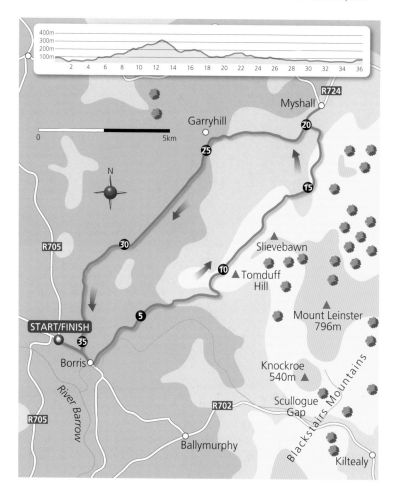

Route Description

This is a route that can be comfortably completed on a summer's evening, with the reward of a visit to one of the local traditional-style public houses. Starting at the top of the bustling village of Borris, continue down to the bottom of the village and turn left, exiting under the sparkling granite viaduct that was once part of the railway line from Bagenalstown to Wexford. Running alongside the road is the Mountain River, a marvellously wild river for much of the year.

The roads are quiet and there is a gradual climb that gets steeper with distance.

The Borris Viaduct at Borris, County Carlow

Two kilometres after the viaduct take a left-hand turn and follow signs for the Mount Leinster Heritage Drive for another 4km. At the crossroads take the left turn, signposted Muine Bheag (as Bagenalstown is also known), followed by another left turn a short few metres away.

The road sweeps around to the right and there is a virtually hidden road on the right around the bend. Turn onto this road and it begins to rise steadily.

The view gets better and better with each metre ascended, rising to 321 metres at its highest.

Local knowledge has it that St Columbanus was born close by here. Columbanus, regarded by many as the 'first European', travelled across the continent founding many monasteries and becoming one of the most influential historical figures in Irish Christianity.

There is hardly ever any traffic up on this road along the side of Slievebawn, which is surprising, given the marvellous views from the top.

The road descends rapidly once the top is crested. Turn right at the next crossroads and follow the signs into the village of Myshall. A visit to the Adelaide Memorial Church is a must. A miniature of Salisbury Cathedral, it was built by John Duguid of Dover in memory of his daughter who was killed in a horse-riding accident while visiting her sister in Myshall.

Leave Myshall by the road you entered the village but continue straight ahead as far as Garryhill and turn left at the crossroads.

Borris is approximately 10km away and the road is flat all the way. Reward yourself with a visit to one of the many fine hostelries in the village.

5. To Arthur's Way and Beyond!

Maynooth – Leixlip – Celbridge – Oughterard Cemetery–
Celbridge – Maynooth

Location: County Kildare

Distance: 41km

Duration: 1½–2 hours

Grade: 2

Height Gain: 219 metres

Verdict: Great route with the family

Start/Finish

Park in the grounds of St Patrick's College Maynooth. Small fee charged.

Saint Patrick's College Maynooth, County Kildare

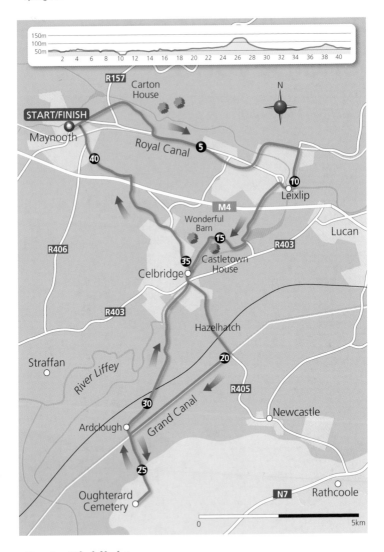

Route Highlights

This is a really pleasant route, rich in history and interesting places, incorporating two short cycles along canal towpaths, two historical houses (the route passes through the grounds of both) and two significant figures from Irish history! It packs in a lot in a short distance and is very convenient to residents of the Dublin commuter belt.

Transport by bike, water and rail – the Royal Canal, near Maynooth, County Kildare

Route Description

Leave Maynooth via the main street and follow Carton Avenue into the grounds of Carton House. Carton House nowadays operates as a four-star hotel and golf resort. Public access is permitted.

Take the right fork just before the bridge on the grounds heading onto the Leixlip–Maynooth road. Cross over the road and swing left onto the Royal Canal towpath (which is excellent for cycling), just to the left of the Pike Bridge.

The canal towpath is a lovely way to avoid traffic on the busy R148 and to travel at a slower pace. On the opposite side of the canal is the railway line and you will probably see a commuter train zipping by with its passengers much quicker than canal barges of the past would have! The Royal Canal alongside Mountjoy Prison was immortalised in song by Brendan Behan in 'The Auld Triangle' in his play *The Quare Fellow*.

I've often felt the canals need to be promoted as greenways out of the city for cyclists – how do you exit Dublin safely with its busy road network?

Stay on the towpath for about 5km, passing Deey Bridge and the reputedly haunted thirteenth lock! The canal starts to curve gently, passing under the Louisa Bridge and your exit is at the next bridge, at Confey.

Pass over the bridge and cycle downhill into Leixlip. Leixlip is one of the fastest growing towns in the country, now very much a satellite of Dublin. It is home to some major multinational companies such as Intel.

The name in Irish, *Léim an Bhradáin*, recognises that the River Liffey was renowned as a salmon fishery.

Of course, before the multinationals located here, there was Guinness, which had its first brewery in Leixlip, so the town can rightfully claim to be the original home of Guinness. Its associations with Guinness are now celebrated in the 14km heritage trail, Arthur's Way, which becomes part of our route.

Follow the road down to the T-junction with Main Street, then turn left and continue as far as the River Liffey Bridge at the Salmon Leap, just to have a peek. Retrace your steps back up Main Street as far as the Spar shop. Turn left into the car park. It is probably best to walk along the riverside path to Main Street, turning left as you emerge.

The road curves to the right but you can take a shortcut up Old Hill. At the top, turn left and stay on the road. You will pass over the M4 after 1km. Just before that you might like to divert to see the unique corkscrew-shaped Wonderful Barn, built in 1743 to store grain.

Continue on the R404 for another kilometre and turn right onto a side road that leads towards Castletown House.

This is another treat as you pass through the 1,100 acres of Ireland's largest Palladian-style house, which was built in 1722. Today the house is in the ownership of the state and is a fantastic resource for the neighbouring towns of Celbridge and Leixlip. There are also cafe facilities attached to the house, making it a perfect stopping point for thirsty cyclists.

Continue through the grounds and enter Celbridge. Keep straight down the main street, passing a statue of Arthur Guinness, who lived here in his early years.

Turn left at the traffic lights and cross over the bridge. Take the right turn (which is straight ahead) off the main road in the direction of Hazelhatch. Cross over the second canal that you encounter today, the Grand Canal, but with caution as this is a narrow humpback bridge on a busy road with poor visibility.

Swing right onto the canal towpath, which has an asphalt surface for the next few kilometres. Hazelhatch has many floating residents so you should see a lot of colourful barges.

This is very easy cycling for 9km on a great surface – and you can even stop off at the Lyons Estate Cafe for another rest stop if you wish. Leave the canal at Henry Bridge (the second bridge after Hazelhatch) and head uphill for 2km before taking a right for Oughterard Graveyard, burial place of Arthur Guinness. There are fine views across Kildare and Meath from the graveyard, which also contains the ruins of a round tower and a church that holds the vaults of the Guinness family, including Arthur himself.

Adding another layer of history is the fact that Daniel O'Connell, 'The Liberator', fought a duel near here in 1815 with John D'Esterre

Castletown House, Celbridge, County Kildare

over criticism O'Connell made of the treatment of the poor by Dublin Corporation. D'Esterre died as a result and O'Connell always regretted this deed.

Another interesting nugget concerns the film *Mission Impossible*. In the film Tom Cruise's character is told that the American president is unavailable 'because he is fishing in Oughter Ard, County Kildare'. The only waterway here is the Grand Canal and I don't think he would have caught much more than a cold here!

This is the outer limit of our route. We return back down the hill to the canal but cross over this time and turn right into the village of Ardclough and follow the road back into Celbridge. Turn left (to rejoin the road on which you exited Maynooth) and cross over the river, then turn right onto Main Street. Turn left onto the Maynooth Road close to the entrance to Castletown House. Stay on the road for 1.5km and take the second left onto Kilgowan Lane (the first left after Celbridge House pub).

Take the first right-hand turn and follow the main road back into Maynooth to your parking spot in St Patrick's College.

6. Barrow to The Nore Loop

Goresbridge – Skeaughvosteen – Dungarvan – Tullaherrin – Bennettsbridge – Gowran – Goresbridge

Location: County Kilkenny	**Grade:** 3
Distance: 42km	**Height Gain:** 442 metres
Duration: 2–2½ hours	**Verdict:** Loved the rural route!

Start/Finish

Goresbridge is a small village on the Kilkenny side of the River Barrow. Take exit 7, Paulstown, off the M9. Continue along the R448 to Gowran. Turn left on entering Gowran onto the R702. Goresbridge is 5km from Gowran and there are parking spaces on the Carlow side of the bridge at Goresbridge.

Route Highlights

Surprising climb and lengthy downhill make this a route a treat.

Tullaherin Round Tower, County Kilkenny

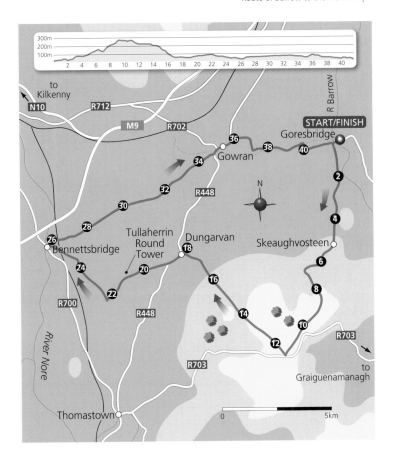

Route Description

Cycle up the main street of the quiet town of Goresbridge and turn left, signposted as Kilkenny Cycle Route No 2. We stay on the route for just 4km before taking a right turn to the wonderfully named Skeaughvosteen.

There is a great climb out of the village, deceptively long but very enjoyable. Go straight across at a crossroads and turn left at the next T-junction, 2km from the village.

There are great views to be had across to Mount Leinster and the Blackstairs as the climb becomes steeper. After 1.5km take the right-hand fork in the road, with good views across towards Brandon Hill. The road narrows and is covered in for a short while by tall conifers in the forestry on top of the hill. You have passed over the highest point here and there is a delightful downhill ahead.

The Ouncel, Dungarvan, County Kilkenny

Turn right at the junction and head back in the direction of the tiny hamlet of Dungarvan. This is a magnificent downhill for 9km and is welcome after the earlier climb.

On reaching Dungarvan, which is on the old Carlow–Waterford road, turn left, passing the attractive frontage of the Ouncel House Bar. Thanks to the M9, this road is no longer heaving with high volumes of traffic; in any event, we turn right off it after just 1km, heading for Tullaherin Round Tower which is just over 2km away.

The round tower comes into views as you draw nearer. The monastic site has a number of ogham stones and a ruined church. A thorough job has been done on identifying the many graves scattered around the church ruins and there is a map clearly identifying each one. It's a nice spot to linger in.

On leaving the site turn right, and in a couple of kilometres you will meet the Kilkenny Cycle Route No. 2 again. Turn right and this will bring you into Bennettsbridge.

Bennettsbridge was bedecked in black-and-amber flags and bunting when I cycled through. Almost every house was festooned with the colours of their hurling heroes. A sight to behold! The village has become a craft hub with nationally renowned craftsmen in pottery, leather, woodturning and candle-making. And, of course, some of the finest exponents of hurling come from Bennettsbridge, such as legendary goalie Noel Skehan (with nine All-Ireland Senior medals), full back Jim Treacy and, from the modern era, Liam Simpson.

We started our journey on the banks of the River Barrow and in Bennettsbridge we are on the banks of its sister river, the Nore.

Take a right-hand turn before the bridge and continue up the hill on the L2656/Gowran road; this is a good flat road to make haste on and you won't be long traversing the 8km or so to Gowran. Gowran is famous for its racetrack and, of course, is the birthplace of hurling wizard D. J. Carey.

There is a ruined church in the town centre, St Mary's Church, which is now a national monument.

You are now on the last leg of this route. Turn right at the top of the town for Goresbridge and it's a slight downhill all the way back to the banks of the Barrow and your car.

Near Skeaughvosteen, County Kilkenny

7. Bilboa and Back

Carlow – Killeshin – Rossmore – Bilboa – Old Leighlin –
Leighlinbridge – Nurney – Tinryland – Carlow

Location: Counties Carlow and Laois

Distance: 44km

Duration: 2½–3 hours

Grade: 3

Height Gain: 519 metres

Verdict: Great climbing onto the Castlecomer plateau on a route rich with interesting stop-offs.

Downhill to Old Leighlin, County Carlow

Start/Finish

Carlow is 100km south-west of Dublin. Take exit 4 off the M9 and follow the R448 to the second roundabout. Turn left onto the N80 (O'Brien Road). Continue to the second roundabout and take the second exit, continuing straight ahead. After 500 metres, turn right and park in the public car park beside Askea Church.

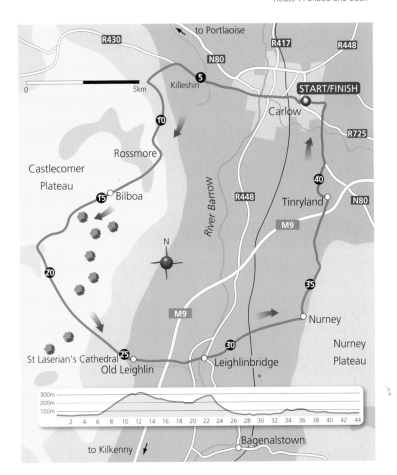

Route Highlights

Carlow town is a great base for exploring the south Leinster region, being a lively, attractive spot with plenty of eateries and accommodation for visiting cyclists. Shortly after leaving Carlow the climb begins and it's a lung-buster to the top of the Castlecomer plateau. On the way up, though, the twelfth-century Romanesque doorway at Killeshin is a must-see. There are fantastic views eastwards from the top. The route is easy going on top of this isolated plateau and the descent down into Old Leighlin is spine-tingling!

St Laserian's Cathedral is one of Ireland's most important ecclesiastical sites (and is Carlow's oldest working building, for it was here that an

Heading uphill to Rossmore, County Laois

important seventh-century church synod took place, which determined the date of Easter for the entire Christian world). Just before the cathedral is St Molaise's Well.

Just down the road from Old Leighlin is picturesque Leighlinbridge, a village with an impressive past and some famous sons, including Captain Myles Kehoe, of the 7th Cavalry who died at the Battle of the Little Bighorn, scientist John Tyndall, one of the most eminent scientists of his time and a pioneer of mountaineering. There are interesting memorial plaques in the riverside garden celebrating these and other distinguished names. The Valerian Bridge across the Barrow is reputed to be one of the oldest in Europe and is guarded by the Black Castle.

Route Description

Leave the car park beside Askea Church and turn right onto the O'Brien Road. At the roundabout take the third exit and cycle through the town centre. Continue straight down the main thoroughfare, Tullow Street, through all the junctions you meet. After 2km you will see Carlow Castle on your left as you pass over the River Barrow.

Keep going out the Castlecomer Road until you arrive at a T-junction just after Fitzpatrick's Pub and opposite the Killeshin community centre. Turn left followed immediately by a right. The climbing begins! It's a lovely ascent and a steady rhythm will take you to the top without much difficulty.

Pass the church on your left and shortly after you will see an older church ruin and graveyard on your right. The famous Killeshin Romanesque doorway is here, a truly remarkable work of art. The climb to the top of the plateau is about 5km.

Romanesque doorway, Killeshin, County Laois

At the top go left followed by a right; this road will bring you across the top of the plateau to the tiny village of Bilboa, once a busy place due to the extensive coalmines on the Castlecomer plateau which were worked for over 300 years from 1640 until the last pit closed in 1969. Nestling between Carlow, Laois and Kilkenny it is now a sparsely populated upland.

It's easy navigate the route up here: just continue to the T-junction 4km beyond Bilboa. Turn left and stay on this road, which continues to rise slightly for another 4km before you meet the exhilarating descent into Old Leighlin.

Just as you come into the hamlet, St Molaise's Well is on the right-hand side on a bend in the road. St Laserian's Cathedral is slightly further ahead and worthy of a visit, especially if the cathedral is open.

Continue down the hill, crossing over the motorway, and head into Leighlinbridge. Pass over the bridge on the River Barrow. There are some great hostelries here in the village and great grub, too, in the Lord Bagenal and the Arboretum.

At the bend in the main street, cross over and take the L3046 up the hill on your left heading for Tullow.

Stay on this road until a staggered junction, where you cross over and up in to the quiet village of Nurney. Turn left in the village onto a road that takes you across to Tinryland village. Pass the church and take a left-hand turn; pass through the next crossroads, continuing on to the main Wexford road, the N80. Turn left and the road brings you back into Carlow town in just 4km.

8. Ring of Hook Bike Route

Duncannon – Hook Head – Tintern Abbey – Duncannon

Location: County Wexford

Distance: 44km

Duration: 2–3 hours

Grade: 2

Height Gain: 326 metres

Verdict: Terrific coastal scenery combined with numerous heritage sites

Start/Finish

Duncannon, south of New Ross, County Wexford. Park at the church.

Route Highlights

A route full of mystery, history and stunning coastal scenery. The Hook Peninsula is now an important stopping-off point in Ireland's Ancient East.

View from the top of Hook Head Lighthouse, County Wexford

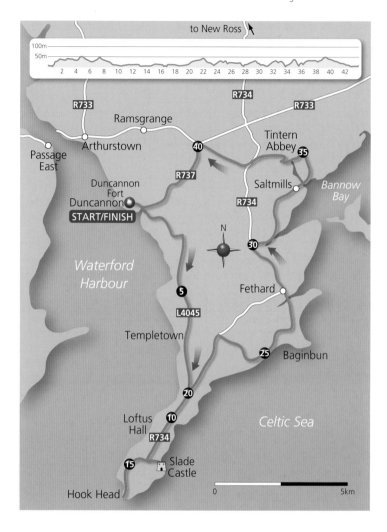

A cycle along the Hook Peninsula is a trip through the ages with many historical sites, including magnificent examples from monastic Ireland and Norman Ireland in particular.

Route Description

Our route begins and ends in the beautiful seaside village of Duncannon, renowned for its fine golden beach where sand sculpting is a popular pastime, attracting local and international sand sculptors. The star-shaped sixteenth-century Duncannon Fort is well worth a visit before setting out on tour.

It's almost impossible to go astray on this route as it consists of one road in and one road out to the Hook Lighthouse. Simply follow the signs for the Ring of Hook Drive on the way down to Hook; the signposts are for the coastal drive, which is slightly different from this bike route thereafter. On leaving Duncannon turn right after 1km onto the L4045. The route is mainly flat but exposed on two sides for much of the trip down the narrow peninsula. There are wonderful views to the right across Waterford Harbour towards Dunmore East and the County Waterford coastline.

Along with the fine views there are a number of interesting sites connected to the Knights Templar worth investigating, for example the Templar church on your right-hand side (across the road form the Templar Inn). The mysterious Templars originated during the Crusades and large tracts of land around Hook were given to the order by King Henry II. The Templars amassed vast wealth and were blamed for the collapse of Christian control of the Holy Land. They were greatly resented for their wealth and power and eventually were rounded up, arrested and the order was dissolved.

The outbound road is easy to navigate: follow the direction signs for the Ring of Hook and before long Ireland's most haunted house

comes into view. Loftus Hall reputedly has a dark and troubled past and tours are available throughout the summer months, if you are brave enough!

Hook Lighthouse is coming more and more into view and is a beacon for tourists as much as it is for seafarers plotting their course along the Wexford coastline. The oldest operational lighthouse in the world now boasts a fantastic visitor centre and cafe, which are open all year round. Keeping watch over Waterford harbour for 800 years, the lighthouse offers guided tours and the views are spectacular from the balcony.

Hook Head, County Wexford

Hook Head, County Wexford

Retrace the road back a couple of kilometres for a quick visit to Slade Castle and harbour, which is well signposted.

Returning on the road that took you down the peninsula, then continue straight ahead towards Fethard-on-Sea, passing by Baginbun 'where Ireland was both lost and won'. The Anglo-Norman invasion of Ireland began with the landing at Baginbun in 1169.

Take the R734 out of Fethard for 2km and turn right onto the L4043. Continue into the village of Saltmills and turn left just before the bridge over the estuary. Tintern Abbey looms ahead in the woodland. The famous Cistercian abbey was built by William Marshal, Earl of Pembroke, around 1200 and was named after Tintern in Wales. After the Dissolution of the Monasteries in the 1540s, the abbey came into the ownership of Anthony Colclough. Situated close by the abbey is the wonderful Colclough Walled Garden which was restored in 2010 and is now a tourist attraction in its own right.

When I completed this tour in 2016 I missed the left-hand turn to Tintern and continued 4km up the L4041 where I managed to reroute by taking the signposted Bannow Bay Walking Trail.

On leaving the Colclough Walled Garden turn left onto a rough track for 1km and exit onto a minor road. This joins the R734 for 500 metres before turning right onto a minor road. Continue on the L8120 for 2km and then turn left onto the R737, which will take you back into Duncannon after 4km and the completion of this fascinating route.

9. Durrow Loop

Durrow – Foyle Bridge – Galmoy – Durrow

Location: Counties Laois and Kilkenny

Distance: 45km

Duration: 2–2½

Grade: 2

Height Gain: 501 metres

Verdict: A tough start but all downhill thereafter!

Start/Finish

A picturesque village located 23km south of Portlaoise, Durrow was a favoured stopping-off point on the old Cork–Dublin road, the N77. Exit the M7 at junction 17 and follow the N77 for about 20km, going through Abbeyleix, to reach Durrow. Park around the green, using the Ashbrook Arms Hotel as your starting point.

River Erkina, Durrow, County Laois

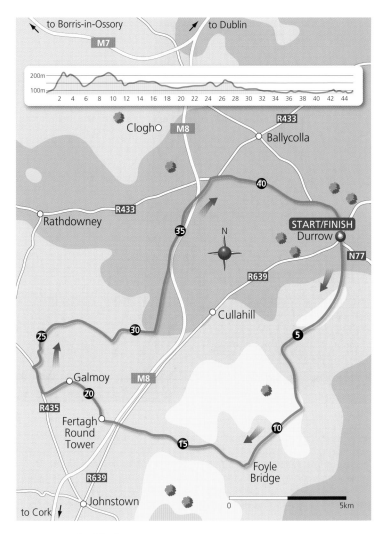

Route Highlights

A cruel 13% gradient at the start of this climb gives the wrong impression of this excellent route on rural back roads straddling Counties Laois and Kilkenny. Good cycling territory.

Route Description

Durrow is a great starting point for this route and indeed many others, as this is prime cycling country. It is a historic town that has improved

Round rower at Fertagh, County Kilkenny

vastly since the motorway took away the heavy traffic and it is a lovely stopping-off point or a base for exploring the region. Durrow Castle is now a beautiful hotel and there are also many walking routes in the area.

This is a very quiet route and you would be advised to bring some refreshments with you as there will not be an opportunity to acquire any en route. It overlaps slightly with official Laois and Kilkenny cycle trails for short distances.

Start at the Ashbrook Arms Hotel. Continue along the street with the green on your right-hand side. Turn left at the end of the street followed by a right shortly afterwards, signposted for Lisdowney.

After the initial shock of the sharp rise you get the full benefit of a good downhill to recover as you glide past some of the fine dairy herds that are so important to the local economy. Glanbia HQ is just a few kilometres away, outside Ballyragget. It is wonderful to see the display of mature native trees along the route here.

As you come down the hill after 5km there is a sharp bend before a crossroads, which you cross and begin a 3km climb. It is not difficult and is the last climbing of the route as it gradually flattens out for the last 20km or so. At a crossroads, turn right along the signposted North Kilkenny Cycle Trail. Stay on this road as far as pretty Foyle Bridge and then turn right towards Gattabawn.

In 6km pass over the busy M8 motorway and continue as far as Fertagh Round Tower, one of the tallest in the country (and possibly the tallest if its capstone were in place). Turn left to enter the tower grounds, otherwise turn right at this T-junction and continue straight through Galmoy to the crossroads with the R435.

Turn right after a kilometre onto a narrow side road that winds its way for 2km, where you go right. Stay on this road, passing through a staggered junction and continue downhill to a T-junction where you turn left. The terrain is very flat now and it is easy to make progress. Go across at a crossroads and turn left at the next crossroads.

Stay on this road, which runs virtually parallel to the motorway. The road passes under the motorway in about 6km and brings you close to Ballacolla. Turn right onto the R433 and then take another quick right onto another narrow side road. This road will bring you back into Durrow by a pleasant riverside pub, An Áitúil, which has a pretty garden on the banks of the Erkina River. Curiously, there is a sign on the wall of the pub for the Nore River. However, the Erkina flows into the Nore a short distance away.

Interesting trivia: the world's largest gathering of high-nelly bicycles, 344, was recorded on this bridge in 2011!

An Áitúil, Durrow, County Laois

10. East Carlow Circuit

Tullow – Ardattin – Ballintemple – Clonegal – Aghowle – Clonmore – Tullow

Location: Counties Carlow and Wicklow

Distance: 52km

Duration: 2½–3 hours

Grade: 4

Height Gain: 611 metres

Verdict: Stunning scenery with some nice climbs

Start/Finish

Tullow is 16km east of Carlow town. It is easily accessed via the N80 from Dublin or the R725 from Carlow. Park in the town car park opposite the municipal buildings.

Cycling on a boreen near Ballintemple, County Carlow

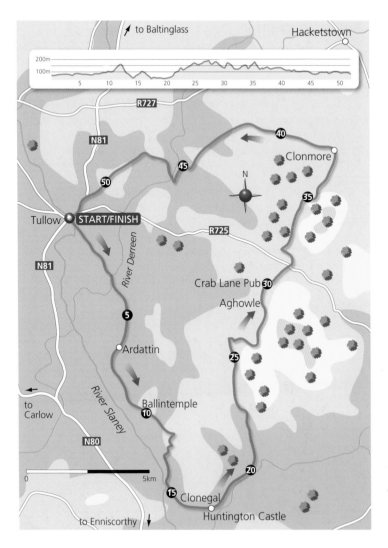

Route Highlights

The roads on this route are exceptionally quiet and the only sound is birdsong as you travel along the Slaney Valley down to Clonegal and onwards to Clonmore. The beauty of this quiet backwater, which really should be a tourist Mecca, will surprise you.

Route Description

Turn left on leaving the car park and leave Tullow behind as you head towards the village of Ardattin 6km away. The road is good and flat and you will speed along this early section.

Turn right in Ardattin followed by a quick left. You are now on a very small boreen that will take you through the townland of Ballintemple and the Coillte nursery. This was once the home of Pierce Butler, a signatory of the American Constitution.

The road runs parallel to the River Slaney here. On the far side of the river and just out of sight is Altamont Gardens, one of Ireland's most important gardens – well worth a diversion if you are so inclined.

As you travel along the road, the grass centre increases in size and the hedgerows crowd in from both sides. It's enchanting. You will eventually meet an equally small road where you turn right and continue to climb a little more.

The views now become spectacular across the Slaney Valley towards Mount Leinster. Kilcarry Bridge is also in view below but take care going downhill here as the road surface deteriorates on this section.

These are views few people see of County Carlow and the route is a real treat. The road meets the L2024 where you turn left to reach Clonegal. But first a quick diversion to Kilcarry Bridge which is 50 metres away on your right: a lovely resting place on the Slaney.

Clonegal has been described as 'the Switzerland of Ireland' because of the surrounding mountains, valleys and rivers. The Slaney and the Derry rivers meet close by at this meeting point of Counties Carlow, Wicklow

View near Kilcarry, Clonegal, County Carlow

and Wexford. The village has twice been awarded the accolade of Ireland's tidiest village, in 2014 and 2015. The displays of flowers every summer are lovely to behold and a great indication of community pride.

A visit to Huntington Castle is a must – *The Guardian* newspaper voted it one of Ireland's top twenty hidden gems in 2015. Guided tours are available, which include the Temple of Isis located in the old castle dungeons. The castle is still lived in by descendants (the Durdin Robertsons) of the original owners (the Esmondes), who were also involved in Duncannon Fort and Johnstown Castle in Wexford.

Retrace your steps to the top of Clonegal village and turn right onto the L6049, following signs for the Wicklow Way. This renowned walking route finishes in Clonegal where the South Leinster Way begins. After 4km turn left, again following the signs for the Wicklow Way. The road begins to rise steadily and this section is part of the official Wicklow Way. The Way heads into the woods 2km further on and we rejoin it shortly after when it comes back to the road.

It's up and down now for a few kilometres but nothing too difficult. The scenery is beautiful in this secluded border area of Carlow and Wicklow. The road is edged by woodland on your right. You will shortly turn right at the next T-junction, again following the signs for the Wicklow Way.

At the next T-junction turn left. We leave the Wicklow Way here and continue along a pleasant scenic road as far Aghowle Church. This is one of the prettiest ruins in the country, situated 400 metres down a laneway. This sixth-century monastery was founded by St Finian.

The wonderfully named Crab Lane Pub is 500 metres away: go right here and continue until you meet the R725. Cross over the staggered junction and go down the hill. At the bottom continue left, followed by a right, and head for Clonmore 5km away.

Clonmore is one of County Carlow's most important Early Christian sites. It is associated with St Mogue who built a monastery here in the sixth century. None of the original buildings survives but there are many important reminders of its past, with two high crosses, a lintel, an ogham stone, two bullaun stones, a font, nineteen cross-inscribed slabs and a holy well.

The village is dominated by the ruins of Clonmore Castle, which was taken by Cromwell in 1650.

Passing the castle we now return to Tullow on good, flat roads. We have an option after 7km to turn right or left – both will take you back to Tullow. Go right and then right again, passing over a bridge, and take the next left. Another left after that and you will eventually join the N81; turning left, you are on the outskirts of Tullow. Cycle through the town and back to car park to finish a very rewarding and challenging route.

11. Johnstown Castle Ring

Johnstown Castle – Kilmore Quay – Our Lady's Island – Johnstown Castle

Location: County Wexford

Grade: 2

Distance: 54km

Height Gain: 289 metres

Duration: 2–2½

Verdict: Quiet country roads of south Wexford

Start/Finish

Car park of Johnstown Castle (small fee). Johnston Castle is just 7 km outside Wexford town. To get there, take the R889 off the N25 route that loops around Wexford town. Be sure to return before closing time.

Tacumshane Windmill, County Wexford

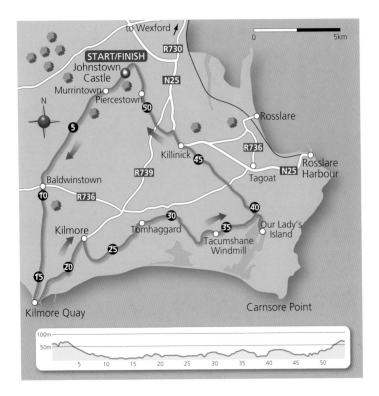

Route Highlights

A ride on the flat is always welcome! While not quite Holland, the presence of the last commercial working windmill in Ireland certainly evokes comparisons with our European neighbour. This relatively short jaunt takes in a hidden corner of County Wexford that has its own delights for the touring cyclist.

Route Description

It is appropriate that the Irish Agricultural Museum is located at the starting point of this route in Johnstown Castle Gardens as the route meanders through a part of Wexford that retains the rural charm of bygone times. The car park in the castle grounds is a good place to use as the starting point for this 54km loop in south Wexford.

Turn left out the gate and go up the slight incline into Murrintown village 2km ahead. It's too early in the cycle for stopping so continue on this quiet road for another 7km, gradually descending, and turn left onto the R738. The road soon intersects the R736: cross over and keep cycling

61

Kilmore village, County Wexford

south, heading for the sea, on this quiet and straight road that leads all the way into famed Kilmore Quay.

This quaint fishing village is a great place to spend a day, with its splendid beach. Boat trips to the Saltee Islands can be booked at the quayside. Kilmore Quay is reputedly home to the best fish-and-chip shop in the country, the Saltee Chipper!

Head out of the village by taking the R739 exit on the roundabout and continue in the direction of Kilmore (not to be confused with Kilmore Quay) and after 3km turn right on to a side road signposted as the Wexford Cycle Route No. 3, on which we travel at various sections. The road meanders east to Tomhaggard. A right-hand turn takes you past a pretty holy well and heading towards Tacumshane Windmill, the last commercial windmill to operate in Ireland. Practically all the timber used in its construction came from driftwood or shipwrecks found on the shoreline close by. It remained in use until 1936 and is now a national monument.

On your right-hand side you can see Our Lady's Island Lake. You soon turn right at the T-junction to arrive in the village of Our Lady's Island, an ancient place of pilgrimage in the Dioceses of Ferns.

Retrace your route back to the T-junction but continue on straight until you arrive in the village of Killinick at which point you must take the busy N25 for just a kilometre. Turn left and head in the direction of Piercestown and the starting point at Johnstown Castle. It's a gentle uphill finish for the last 5km. Take the first exit at the roundabout and the finish point is just ahead on your left.

12. Sallins Loop

Sallins – Prosperous – Donadea – Maynooth – Celbridge – Grand Canal – Sallins

Location: County Kildare

Distance: 55km

Duration: 2½–3 hours

Verdict: Rural treat in the commuter belt

Grade: 2

Height Gain: 256 metres

McEvoy's Pub, Hazlehatch, on the Grand Canal, County Kildare

Start/Finish

Sallins is a small village on the outskirts of Naas, County Kildare. If coming from Dublin, take the N7 and take the slip road for Naas in view of one of Ireland's most iconic pieces of public art – officially titled 'Perpetual Motion' but known better as 'the Naas Ball'. Take the second exit off the first and second roundabouts, which will take you onto the L2012, Monread Road. Take the third exit at the next roundabout onto the R407, which will bring you into Sallins. Park beside the Grand Canal in the village.

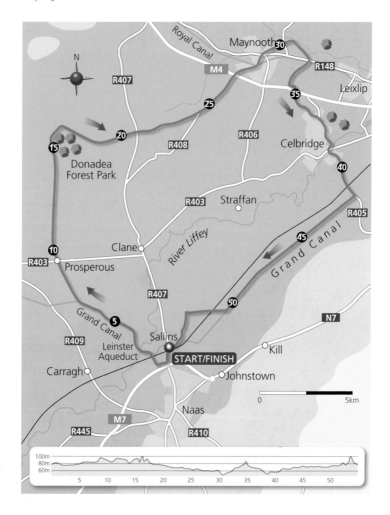

Route Highlights

When I think of Kildare I think of motorways criss-crossing the county and heavy traffic volumes bound for the capital city. Thankfully, the county has a network of quiet, rural roads that open up the delights of a county packed with interesting sights. This route takes in gentle canal vistas and towpaths and a surprising variety of terrain, from bog to the immaculate stud farms of the Thoroughbred County. A quiet cycle in the commuter belt!

Route Description

The route begins in Sallins, a dormitory town on the edge of Naas. Park beside the Grand Canal on Millbank Road.

We follow the canal in the early stages but do so on the opposite bank, therefore it is necessary to head in the direction of Naas, taking a right turn after 800 metres onto Osborne Cottages followed by a second right turn that will bring you alongside the left bank of the Grand Canal.

The canal passes over the River Liffey via the Leinster Aqueduct. This imposing four-arched bridge was constructed over 200 years ago and is still an impressive sight. The building of the canals was a massive engineering feat and they quickly became important arteries of trade during the Industrial Revolution. Canals have, of course, been in existence since early civilisations in Egypt and China.

The road shadows the canal for the next 5km, passing by Digby Bridge and Lock Gates. The route crosses over at Landenstown Bridge to the opposite bank with the road veering away from the canal in the direction of Prosperous. This village was one of the first places where the United Irishmen rose in 1798 and there is an interesting memorial to Ruth Hackett who was killed in the Battle of Prosperous.

Cross the main road, the R403, in the village; the memorial is on your left. After leaving the village take the right-hand fork in the road and onto a long straight stretch, passing bogland on your right.

Go straight across at a crossroads. Donadea Forest Park is located on the right-hand side and is bordered by an impressive wall. Keep the park on your right shoulder, veer right at another fork in the road and take the

Barge on the Grand Canal, near Sallins, County Kildare

next right. The entrance to Donadea Park is a short distance ahead, but continue past. Turn left onto Barberstown Road and cross over the R407 in another kilometre onto the L1010. When it meets the R408, turn left. This road can be busy as you approach Maynooth, which is 4km distant, crossing over the M4.

Maynooth is an attractive university town with plenty of stopping-off points for refreshments and sightseeing. NUI Maynooth is Ireland's newest university, founded in 1997 when it separated from the much older St Patrick's College Maynooth (founded 1795).

The route continues along the main street before joining the wonderful Carton Avenue, which links the town with Carton House.

Carton House is a beautifully restored historic mansion, now a four-star hotel and golf resort. The estate first came into the ownership of the Fitzgeralds in 1170 and the first record of a house at Carton was in the seventeenth century. The current house came into being in the mid 1700s. Public access is permitted and it is a nice 4km route to exit the town as you head for Celbridge.

Exit Carton House and cross over a second canal – the Royal Canal. Not too often one cycles over two different canals on the same day in Ireland!

Follow the road ahead until it meets the R405, turn left and again cross over the M4.

Do not follow the left-turn signposts for Celbridge but continue straight and take the next left which allows you to enter the town by a quieter road, bordered on both sides by beautiful stud farms and well-maintained hedgerows.

Continue to the main street, passing a statue of Arthur Guinness who had close associations with the town.

Turn left, crossing over the River Liffey, and take the right-hand turn (which is straight ahead) off the main road in the direction of Hazelhatch.

After 3km approximately the road takes you past Hazelhatch train station. A quaint country pub, McEvoys, comes into view on the left just before the humpback bridge over the Grand Canal. Go over the bridge – but with extreme caution as this is a narrow bridge on a busy road with poor visibility – and turn right onto the canal towpath.

Dozens of barges and boats are moored along the canal here, some of them overgrowing with vegetable and flower gardens!

The towpath is really well surfaced for the next 3km at which point you arrive at the Lyons Estate and the pretty Canal Cafe, a nice stopping-off point.

Shortly afterwards, you encounter the thirteenth lock, the gates of which are reputedly haunted. It is claimed the canal was laid through an old graveyard, and drivers of horses pulling boats in the early days of the canal often reported being accompanied by a ghostly presence. Canal boatmen would never moor their boats near this lock.

The canal towpath is good as far as Ponsonby Bridge, but from there on, the surface deteriorates although it is good enough to cycle on. Continue on the towpath for 2km to Devonshire Bridge and cross over.

Stay on the road for 2km, passing over a railway line until you reach a crossroads.

Another worthwhile diversion presents itself here as you can continue straight on to the grave of Theobald Wolfe Tone in Bodenstown. Wolfe Tone, one of the leaders of the United Irishmen, was a key figure in Irish history.

But if you are not inclined, take a left-hand turn to return to Sallins 2km distant.

Leinster Aqueduct carrying the Grand Canal over the River Liffey, County Kildare

13. The Bog of Allen Circuit

Rathangan – Edenderry – Clogharinka – Carbury – Derrinturn – Allenwood – Lullymore – Rathangan

Location: Counties Kildare and Offaly

Distance: 56km

Duration: 2½–3 hours

Grade: 2

Height Gain: 230 metres

Verdict: Flat route through the Bog of Allen.

On the Bog of Allen, County Kildare

Start/Finish

Rathangan is 10km north of Kildare town. Park on the main street.

Route Highlights

The Bog of Allen is a vast area stretching into Counties Kildare, Offaly, Laois and Meath. It is a raised bog and one of Ireland's most important peatlands, a unique part of our natural heritage. It's one of those places we have all heard of but probably never visited. This is a great route to explore the area and, with flat roads, it is an easy circuit.

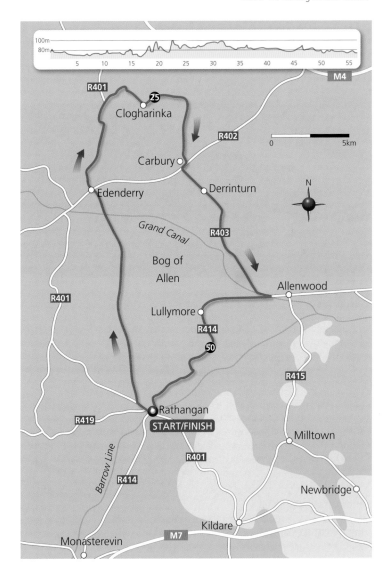

Route Description

Head out of the busy market town of Rathangan in the direction of Edenderry. When you reach the roundabout there are two options for Edenderry: take the third exit across the Bog of Allen. This is the quieter option. Follow the road all the way to Edenderry 13km distant.

69

Rail tracks on the Bog of Allen, County Kildare

There are fantastic panoramic views across the bog towards the Hill of Allen on your right. You can see the narrow-gauge rail tracks that criss-cross the bog and are used by Bord na Móna to transport the milled peat.

Much of the bog has been depleted and it is expected that most of the peat-fired electricity stations will be closed in the coming decades and the bogs will become wildlife preserves.

As you approach Edenderry you will pass under what must be the smallest bridge in the country. Locally called 'The Tunnel', it is in fact the Blunder Aqueduct, which carries the Grand Canal over the road.

Continue to the T-junction and turn left onto Fr Kearns Street. Turn right after 300 metres onto the R401, the Kinnegad road.

I was taken by surprise to see the road cross over the River Boyne about 2km outside the town.

There are a couple of short, steep inclines just ahead and keep an eye out for Carrickoris Castle on the right-hand side as you puff and pant on the steepest of these small rises.

There is a marked contrast in the scenery around here with lots of native trees and beautiful drumlins that are a welcome sight after the big-sky country on the Bog of Allen.

Our route takes a right fork after 1.2km onto the L5009, heading for the small village of Clogharinka. Keep an eye out for the herds of alpacas beside this road!

At the T-junction in Clogharinka turn right onto some lovely easy cycling roads as the loop turns south towards Carbury. In 2km turn left (either direction will take you to Carbury).

Carbury is a pretty little village and a nice resting point. The roads have been reconfigured around the village but it's nicer to cycle through and cross the R402 through a pedestrian walkway and follow the R403 via Derrinturn to the outskirts of Allenwood.

Take a sharp right turn over the Grand Canal onto the R414 heading for Lullymore.

Lullymore Heritage and Discovery Park is well worth a visit, featuring beautiful gardens, woodland walks and historical exhibitions. It provides a great insight into the raised bogs of the midlands and the flora and fauna of the area.

Continue on the road past Lullymore for 9km to return to Rathangan and the completion of a unique cycle route.

On the Grand Canal near Edenderry, County Offaly

14. Vicarstown/ Emo Circuit

Vicarstown – Emo – The Heath – Rock of Dunamase – Athy – Vicarstown

Location: Counties Laois and Kildare

Distance: 56km

Duration: 2½–3 hours

Grade: 2

Height Gain: 327 metres

Verdict: Great cycling country with excellent surfaces

Start/Finish

Exit the M7 at Junction 15 onto the L3930 to reach Vicarstown, which is 16km east of Portlaoise and roughly the same distance north-east of Athy. Park in the car park opposite the 250-year-old Vicarstown Inn.

Vicarstown, County Laois

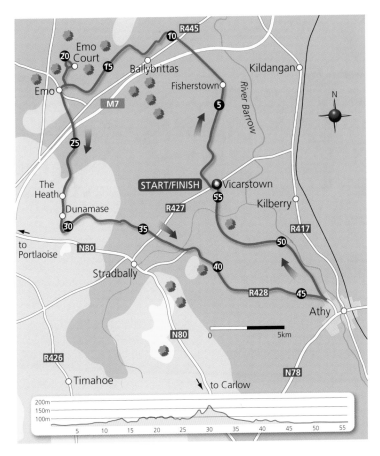

Route Highlights

The circuit is located in a quiet, rural corner of Counties Laois and Kildare. It's a wonderfully gentle cycle on excellent local roads and has some fascinating stopping-off points. Vicarstown, home to Barrowline Cruisers, is better known to canal lovers than touring cyclists but it is the perfect starting point for this pleasant route.

Route Description

Leave Vicarstown with the Inn on your right. At the T-junction turn right, then pass Annanough GAA Club on your left. The road is very flat and well surfaced, great for cruising!

Take another right onto the L3932 along a quiet back road that reaches the beautiful Fisherman's Inn after 5km. It's a very tempting spot to stop off

Emo Court, County Laois

but with another 50km to go, its advisable to keep those wheels turning! Further on the road you will pass Courtwood GAA field on your right and shortly afterwards the road passes over the M7. It begins to rise ever so slightly thereafter.

In another kilometre cross over the slightly staggered crossroads with the R445 and continue on to the next crossroads where you turn right. Shortly after, turn left at the next crossroads, heading in the direction of Ballybrittas.

At the next T-junction, turn right followed by a left, which will bring you onto the road leading to Emo Court Demesne.

Emo Court is a beautiful Gandon-designed mansion with attractive gardens and a café: a welcome place to break the journey.

Turn left when exiting Emo Court, then turn right in the direction of the M7 and a short distance ahead turn right onto a minor road which will bring you to the R445. Turn right onto it and then take a left-hand turn and cycle over the M7 heading in the direction of the Heath. The plain of the Heath is a much smaller version of the Curragh, with sheep roaming freely.

Just ahead are the beautiful wooded hills surrounding the Rock of Dunamase. The road begins to rise on the approach to the impressive hilltop castle ruins that were once the home of the O'Moores of Laois. It's an impressive sight from all sides and worth walking up through the extensive ruins to enjoy the view from the top.

Leave the Rock and keep left to follow the road along the contour of the adjoining hill. At the next crossroads, continue straight ahead until you arrive at a T-junction. Turn left, followed by a quick right and follow the road as far as the intersection with the R427 (which is a shorter return to the starting point, if you need to curtail your tour). Cross over and continue until you meet the main R428 where you turn left for Athy. This can be a busy stretch for the next 10km but it is good and flat and you will speed along. On approaching Athy turn left onto a road parallel to the Barrow Line of the Grand Canal. This is a lovely way to finish the route with the canal on your left and little or no traffic for the last 10km.

The Bluebell Wood at Emo Court, County Laois

15. Carlow Town Loop

Carlow – Milford – Ballinabranna – Rossmore – Ballickmoyler – Maganey – Tinryland – Carlow

Location: Counties Carlow, Laois and Kildare

Distance: 58km

Duration: 2½–3 hours

Grade: 3

Height Gain: 466 metres

Verdict: Great views of the Barrow Valley and a nice climb

Milford Bridge, Milford, County Carlow

Start/Finish

Carlow is 100km south-west of Dublin. Exit the M9 at Junction 4 and follow the R448 to the second roundabout. Turn left onto the N80 (the O'Brien Road). Continue to the second roundabout and take the second exit, continuing straight ahead. After 500 metres, turn right and park in the public car park beside Askea Church.

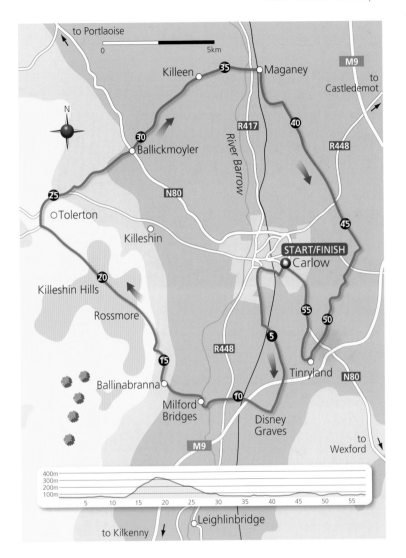

Route Highlights

Never more than 15km from Carlow town centre, this route provides great views of the town and the Barrow Valley from Rossmore. This circuit is on lovely quiet roads all the way around. It packs in some interesting sights – including a visit to the last resting place of Walt Disney's ancestors. The Disneys left Clonmelsh in 1834 for New York but there are three of Walt's

Rossmore, County Laois

ancestors buried here. Also buried in this graveyard are the family of Pierce Butler, one of the signatories of the American Constitution.

The stunning Milford Bridges on the River Barrow are a much-admired scenic and favourite venue for wedding photographs. Carlow was the first town in Ireland to be fully electrified, with electricity generated at Milford Mills in 1891.

A nice climb through the village of Ballinabranna up the Killeshin Hills to Rossmore is rewarded with magnificent views of Carlow town, the Barrow Valley, Mount Leinster and the Wicklow Mountains in the distance.

Route Description

After turning right onto the O'Brien Road from the car park at Askea Church, take the second exit at the roundabout and continue straight ahead as far as Éire Óg GAA Club. Take the third exit at the roundabout in front of the club, cycling under the railway bridge. Cross over the River Burrin and pass Woodies on your left. Take the next left onto Hanover Road. At the roundabout take the first exit onto Blackbog Road, which will take you out of town.

The road goes through a railway crossing and at the T-junction, go right. Pass over the M9 and at the next T-junction turn right.

If you want to visit the Disney graves, turn left after 400 metres and cycle down this side road for another 500 metres to the graveyard. Return to the T-junction and go left to resume the route.

The road passes over the M9 once more and, shortly after, the railway line. The road meets the old Carlow–Kilkenny road, the still-busy R448. Go across the staggered junction and soon you will arrive at Milford Bridges. It is well worth getting off and having a look around this popular picnic spot.

The road passes over two bridges. At Alexanders' stud farm turn right at the junction, followed by a left, which is signposted for Ballinabranna.

The climb begins here and continues for 6km. It is a easy gradient as far as the GAA grounds but it steepens pretty quickly thereafter and there is a good workout ahead for the next twenty-five minutes or so.

If you can keep the sweat from trickling into your eyes, you will be rewarded with stunning views along the climb to Rossmore.

The viewing point at the top is a good excuse to stop and recover. The statue in the grotto here was one of the famous 'moving statues' in 1985 when the country experienced a phenomenon that swept the nation!

Continue straight along the plateau past the old Rossmore collieries. The road soon begins to descend and it's freewheeling for 5km to the junction with the R431/Carlow–Castlecomer road. Turn right and continue cycling back towards Carlow for 3km, passing Behans of Tolerton, a popular watering hole.

Take a side road to your left, the L7893 for Ballickmoyler, on a bend on the main road. This will bring you into the small village of Ballickmoyler, crossing the N80.

Follow signs for Killeen and Maganey. Just before Maganey, you pass over the River Barrow and meet the Athy–Carlow road. Cross it and head up the short hill, then turn right. Continue on this road, crossing a humpback bridge over the River Lerr. Stay left at the junction, ignoring the sign for Carlow. This is a pleasant road all the way to the junction with the main Carlow–Dublin road, the R448. This is a staggered junction, which you cross, then cycle uphill, heading over to Rutland Church. Turn right here and continue in the direction of Bennekerry. The road soon passes Palatine GAA club. Exit onto the R725, turning right at Kernanstown and then left after a few hundred metres.

Continue past Dan Morrissey's Quarrying HQ, over the River Burrin, followed by an immediate right and then a left at the top of the hill.

The route continues on good roads across to the village of Tinryland, where there is a window in the local church dedicated to the memory of Captain Myles Kehoe (or Keogh) who fought and died at the Battle of the Little Bighorn.

It is a short 3km back into Carlow town.

16. Abbeyleix and Wolfhill Route

Abbeyleix – Ballinakill – Castlecomer – Clogh – The Swan –
Wolfhill – Ballyroan – Abbeyleix

Location: Counties Laois and Kilkenny

Distance: 58km

Verdict: Packs in some great scenery!

Duration: 2½–3 hours

Grade: 3

Height Gain: 517 metres

Start/Finish

To reach Abbeyleix, exit the M7 at Junction 17 and turn left at the top of the slip road. Follow the N77 for about 12km. Park on the main street or around the square.

Masslough, Ballinakill, County Laois

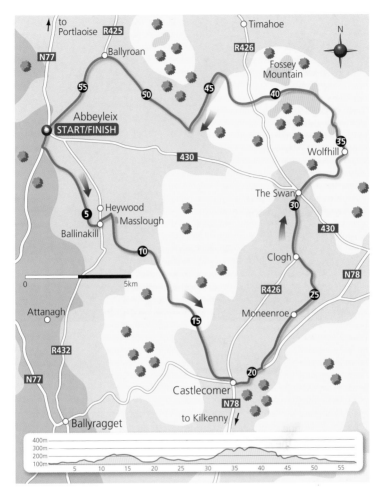

Route Highlights

Masslough, on the edge of Ballinakill, is hidden away from view and what a stunning lake it is! The views from Wolfhill and Fossey Mountain are breathtaking in all directions and the roads are great for cycling.

Route Description

Abbeyleix, bypassed by the M7 in 2010, is one of the oldest planned estate towns in Ireland. The work of Viscount de Vesci, there is a tremendous built heritage to explore. One famous stopping-off point is Morrisey's Bar, built in 1770. Situated on the main street, it is one of Ireland's favourite pubs. A must-visit, but probably better to complete the route first!

Wolfhill, County Laois

Cycle down the main street, with Morrissey's on your right-hand side. Rather than take the main route to Ballinakill, which is winding and dangerous, there is a safer alternative just on the edge of town, off the N77. Turn left onto the L5731, which will bring you to the edge of Ballinakill. After 5km turn left onto the L5735, which takes you into the village. Continue up the main street through the square where there is a monument to the 1798 Rebellion. Take a right-hand turn, signposted as Laois Cycle Route A.

This road turns back around the village past an entrance to beautiful Heywood Gardens and around the Masslough road.

The lake appears as if by magic, one of the best-kept secrets in Laois. When I visited, it was a classic autumnal scene – a semicircular silver lake, bordered on three sides by native woodland and a riot of autumn colours. The sun burst through just as I stopped and the colours became even brighter reds and yellows and golden browns. The only sounds were of the abundant birdlife on the lake, including swans, ducks and herons on the far side. I would have stayed all day but it was time to move on!

Continue past the lake and the wood and turn left at a T-junction (ignoring the signs for the Laois Cycle Route), then a right shortly after onto the L5732 as far as Ironmills Bridge. Turn sharp left onto the L1738 and continue on to the L1829 all the way into Castlecomer, turning right at the junction on the edge of town.

Proceed into the square and turn left. Continue to the end of the town and out past Castlecomer Discovery Park.

Pass the Ormonde Brick Factory and turn left on to the L5874. The road runs straight for about 4km, parallel to the N78. Continue into the village of Clogh. This is quite a populated area with houses scattered across the plain; most people in the area would have been employed in the collieries in times past. Pass through Clogh and onto the 'new village' of The Swan. The village was built after the opening of the Flemings Fireclay factory in 1935. Flemings provided all the houses in the village until 2003 when two new developments took place. The factory is now owned by Lagan Brick.

Cross this dangerous crossroads with care and continue up the hill for 3km to the top and turn left at the sign for Wolfhill Church. The views across Laois, Carlow and Wicklow are spectacular on a clear day.

Continue past the church and on the descent make a left-hand turn onto the L3850. Turn left after 2km at the next crossroads onto a heavily wooded road and continue as far as the crossroads with the R426, The Swan–Timahoe Road. Cross over and continue downhill but be careful as the surface here is not good. Turn left at the T-junction and proceed for 3km to another crossroads where you turn right. The L7780 will bring you into the village of Ballyroan where you turn left onto the R425, which takes you back into Abbeyleix.

17. Ballitore/Glen of Imaal Circuit

Ballitore – Grangecon – Stratford-on-Slaney – Castleruddery
– Knockanarrigan – Glen of Imaal – Donard – Dunlavin –
Narraghmore – Ballitore

Location: Counties Kildare and Wicklow

Distance: 59km

Verdict: Head for the hills!

Duration: 3–3½ hours

Grade: 3

Height Gain: 618 metres

Lugnaquilla from the Glen of Imaal, County Wicklow

Start/Finish

To reach the tiny Quaker village of Ballitore exit the M9 at Junction 3 and take the R747 to a T-junction. Turn left onto the R448, then left again onto Ballitore Hill. Park anywhere around the village and face your bike for the Wicklow Hills.

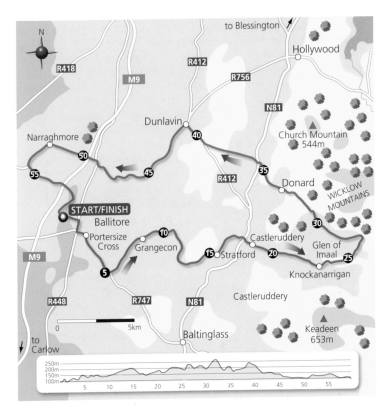

Route Highlights

Any route that takes in mountain scenery and quaint villages is sure to be interesting and this does not disappoint. In 1685 two Quakers decided to settle beside the River Griese and thus began the village of Ballitore. Over the next 200 years more Quakers arrived and developed what became known as the Quaker village.

The Quaker heritage is still alive and celebrated in Ballitore following a revival over the last twenty years with the refurbishment of the Old Meeting House and the rebuilding of Mary Leadbeater's house, which now contains a library and Quaker museum.

This unique village is a terrific starting point for a route that journeys across the county boundary into the wild and rugged Glen of Imaal, one of my favourite places in the Garden County.

Route Description

Starting with Mary Leadbeater's House on your left, continue out to the main road and turn right onto the R448 followed quickly by a left turn onto the R747 in the direction of Baltinglass. Continue through the signposted Portersize Crossroads and straight on at the next crossroads before turning left at a T-junction. Shortly after that continue straight on to a minor road in the direction of Grangecon just over 2km ahead. The approach to the village is picturesque with fine stud farms and beautiful mature trees bordering the roadside.

Grangecon is a strong horse-breeding area with number of successful stud farms in the locality. It is a beautiful area of low, rolling hills. The village once had a railway station but the line was closed in 1959.

Turn right in the village and continue to a T-junction 2km distant where you turn right. Continue around the contour of Ballyhook Hill for 4km to the village of Stratford-on-Slaney. There are great views across to the Wicklow Mountains with Keadeen and Lugnaquilla looming ahead.

Stratford was once a thriving town of over 3,000 before the Great Famine. Now the population is around 300. It has a significant industrial history with cotton and linen works located here.

Continue downhill to the bridge over the River Slaney and cross the main N81, heading up a short, steep hill. Castleruddery stone circle is on your right-hand side and worth visiting. The circle consists of forty stones, some decorated with cup marks while two enormous white quartz portal stones, each weighing at least 15 tons, mark the entrance.

You are now entering the Glen of Imaal and the road continues for 9km deep into the glen. It's a wonderful cycle route with mountains on both sides, Keadeen towering on the right and the North Prison of Lugnaquilla dominating the skyline ahead. Navigation is simple: continue

Glen of Imaal, County Wicklow

straight, heading for 'Lug', on the way passing through Knockanarrigan and in front of Coolmoney Camp. The Glen of Imaal has been used as an army artillery range since 1900 and is at the centre of Irish army peacekeeping preparations. There are many warning signs here not to leave the public roads and it is best to comply.

Continue past Fentons Pub, which is a popular parking spot for hillwalkers who climb Lugnaquilla from here, and over the River Slaney again at Seskin Bridge. Just up the small hill on the right-hand side is a wonderful memorial to the sixteen soldiers who were killed here in an accidental explosion in 1941. There are sixteen granite stones arranged in a semicircle around a central standing stone which has a plaque bearing the names of those who died in that awful accident.

Continue past the memorial, passing Cemetery Hill which is on your right. The views across to Lugnaquilla are breathtaking here. Turn left at a T-junction and the road winds its way for 6km up hill to the pretty village of Donard at the other end of the glen. Take a slight right in the village and continue downhill past the mountain-rescue centre on your left until the junction with the N81 at the Olde Tollhouse Pub.

Cross over and continue on a largely straight road through beautiful rolling countryside for 3km, turning slightly right at a Y-junction onto the R412 shortly before Dunlavin.

Dunlavin is a village with unusually wide streets and a beautiful courthouse built in the Doric style, one of only three such buildings in Ireland. Interestingly, the church is dedicated to St Nicholas of Myra, a saint we meet on another route in County Kilkenny at Jerpoint, where he is reputedly buried. He is considered to be the original Santa Claus.

Continue straight ahead. The road swings sharply left. Continue out of the village, passing Rathsallagh House after 4km. Veer right at the next Y-junction and turn right at another T-junction, just before Colbinstown Bridge. Shortly after, go right, following a signpost for the 'Main Road'. You could continue straight ahead for a shorter return to Ballitore but this is a quieter road and will bring you towards Narraghmore.

Cycling a bike must be similar to horseback journeys of old; the speed is slow, you are elevated and have time to see your surroundings in great detail.

Turn right at the junction with the R448, followed quickly by a left heading up to Narraghmore. On the way up, just after the local athletic track, there is a well called the Drummerswell. A memorial stone records the 'Drummer Boy killed here at the battle of the Pikebridge in 1798'. It's one of those gems you will never see while travelling by car.

Continue up to the top of the hill and turn left for Ballitore. Continue as far as the signposted Chuckle's Crossroads where you turn left, heading in the direction of Crookstown. Just before Crookstown, veer right and you will return to the starting point in just over a kilometre.

18. On the Trail of the Saints

St Mullins – Drummond – Poulmounty Bridge – Inistioge – Graiguenamanagh – Ullard Church – Borris – St Mullins

Location: Counties Carlow, Wexford and Kilkenny

Distance: 61km

Verdict: Good climbing and great views

Duration: 3–3½ hours

Grade: 4

Height Gain: 817 metres

View of the Barrow near New Ross, County Wexford

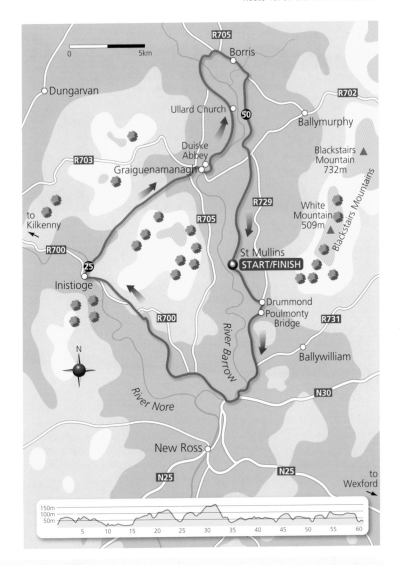

Start/Finish

St Mullins sits at the southernmost tip of County Carlow, 15km north of New Ross. Take the N30 out of New Ross heading towards Enniscorthy. Turn left onto the R729 to Drummond and turn left onto L3008 to St Mullins. Park anywhere near the motte.

River Barrow at Graiguenamangh Quay, County Kilkenny

Route Highlights

This route visits four of the prettiest villages in Ireland. The Barrow and the Nore are sister rivers and these towns are closely associated with the rivers, and all are places steeped in historical significance. Saints Moling, Fiacre and Columba are all connected with the area. This truly is a hidden corner of Ireland best explored by bicycle. The roads are good and mostly quiet with plenty of ascents and descents to give it a real bite.

Route Description

Stunning St Mullins was an important monastic settlement as significant as Clonmacnoise and Glendalough. There are extensive monastic ruins, the famous St Moling's well and a large mound – the remains of a Norman motte and bailey – beside the cemetery. The cemetery contains the graves of many insurgents from the 1798 Rebellion and down by the river are the remains of flour and woollen mills. A short stroll around before starting your cycle is recommended.

Starting at the gates of the graveyard, cycle past An Siopa Glas and take an immediate right turn, heading for Drummond. There is a severe early climb for about a kilometre that will prove an early test for what is to come later!

Keep straight and join the New Ross Road (R729) at Drummond and freewheel down to Poulmounty Bridge, the southernmost tip of County Carlow bordering both Counties Wexford and Kilkenny.

As you climb the hill heading in the direction of New Ross there are some great views of the heavily wooded sides of the Barrow Gorge. In about 6km you will meet the Wexford–New Ross road, a busy section but you are on it for only 800 metres.

Take a right-hand turn signposted for Kilkenny and Graiguenamanagh and cross over the River Barrow. Less than 2km away the Barrow and Nore meet to flow on towards Waterford where they merge with the Suir to form 'The Three Sisters'.

Take a sharp left after the bridge and continue for 1.5km on the R700, which can be busy at certain times. You can then cycle straight ahead onto a traffic-free minor road. This cycle stays on minor roads for the next 6km. Take the next right and, at the next Y-junction, keep right. At the next T-junction turn left – you will see the main road to your right but ignore it.

The road meets the R700 at a bend. Rejoin the R700 heading for Inistioge but follow the Kilkenny Cycle Trail signs and make a right-hand turn off the main road. This helps avoid the traffic and will bring you right into Inistioge.

Cross over the bridge. There is a lovely riverside park here on the banks of the Nore and it's an ideal resting point.

Inistioge has been a very popular destination over the years, especially with fishermen and walkers. There are some lovely pubs and restaurants and there is a historic walk which is well worth following if time permits. Woodstock Gardens have been restored and are proving a big draw for visitors. The local GAA pitch alongside the banks of the River Nore must have one of the most scenic locations in the country.

Suitably rested, retrace your route across the bridge. Do not take the first left but the next one around the bend, onto the L4209 signposted for Graiguenamanagh.

The surface is good and the road is quiet but there is a 7km hill to tackle; however, the fine views across County Kilkenny make it pass quickly. Once the top is reached the reward is a swift descent into Graiguenamanagh and stunning vistas across to the Blackstairs and County Carlow.

Graigue is a Mecca for boat enthusiasts and the quayside is a sight with barges and pleasure craft moored along both banks of the River Barrow. The village gets its name from the monks of what was once Ireland's largest Cistercian abbey, Duiske (Graiguenamanagh is an anglicisation of *Gráig na Manach* – village of the monks). Every approach road to the village and even on the Barrow Track celebrates the association with the abbey with beautiful individual granite statues of monks in various poses.

With its diving boards on the quay Graigue is a popular swimming spot on the Barrow and could be a good place to take a refreshing dip if time permits!

With the entrance to Duiske Abbey on your right, continue up the hill and follow this road as far as the twelfth-century Ullard Church 4km distant. The monastery here is associated with Saints Moling and Fiacre, the latter being one of the renowned Irish missionaries to France and patron saint of gardeners. Beautifully located with the Blackstairs as a backdrop, it is well worth a visit. The Romanesque doorway is a fine example of its type and is said to feature both St Moling and St Fiacre in a

Downhill into Graiguenamanagh, County Kilkenny

panel of the doorway. At the back of the church is a high cross and a most unexpected sight: a handball alley built onto the gable wall!

Moving on, when the road meets the Borris road, turn right and follow the directional signs for one of Carlow's prettiest villages. After crossing over the River Barrow at Ballytiglea Bridge there is a short climb to a T-junction. Turn right and pedal down Borris's main street with its traditional shopfronts and olde-worlde bars/hardware stores. Borris House is on the opposite side of the road and has an amazing history. The ancestral home of the McMurrough Kavanaghs, High Kings of Leinster, is owned by Sara and Morgan Kavanagh, the sixteenth generation of the family. It occupies the most stunning location, high above the banks of the River Barrow, commanding views of Mount Leinster and the Blackstairs Mountains while surrounded by old woodland and gardens.

Borris has become a very popular destination and is the centre of Carlow tourism.

Cycle down the pretty main street of Borris, with its granite cottages and walls, out past the impressive Borris Viaduct. The viaduct is a mighty creation and has now been turned into a popular loop walk. Its sixteen granite arches span the picturesque valley of the Mountain River, a tributary of the Barrow.

With the viaduct on your left go uphill and continue on this road for 5km to the viewing point above Clashganny. This is probably the most photographed stretch of the River Barrow, directly above Clashganny lock and weir with Borris visible in the distance.

Resume your journey and at the next T-junction take the right turn towards Graiguenamanagh. After about 300 metres take the side road which continues straight ahead at the crossroads. This little side road will take you all the way back to St Mullins which is just 7km away.

19. Rebel River Route

Rathvilly – Clonmore – Hacketstown – Kiltegan – Rathangan –
Glen of Imaal – Baltinglass – Rathvilly

Location: Counties Carlow and Wicklow

Distance: 64km

Duration: 3–3½ hours

Grade: 4

Height Gain: 678 metres

Verdict: Quiet roads on a lovely scenic route

Start/Finish

The County Carlow village of Rathvilly on the N81 is the starting point for this cycle. Park at the GAA Club where there are plenty of parking spaces.

Route Highlights

This route takes in some delightful countryside, spectacular mountain scenery, historic villages and recalls some important historical figures from the area.

Leafy canopy at Tuckmill, Baltinglass, County Wicklow

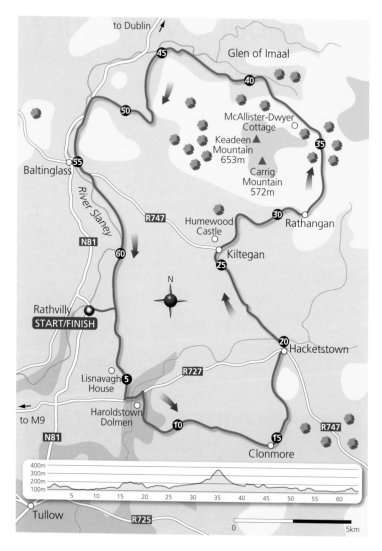

Route Description

A three-time winner of the national Tidy Towns title in the 1960s, Rathvilly is a pretty village in north-east Carlow. Pedalling around this quiet corner of Carlow and into west Wicklow, I was intrigued by the fascinating history of local patriots and of the local big houses. Rathvilly has always been proud of its connection with Kevin Barry who went to school in the village. His parents were from the Hacketstown area and Kevin was immortalised

Heading into the Glen of Imaal from Rathdangan, County Wicklow

in ballad following his hanging in Mountjoy by British forces during the War of Independence. He was arrested after a gun battle on the streets of Dublin in which three British soldiers were killed – the first soldiers to be killed since 1916.

After parking, cycle back into the village and turn right, heading uphill as far as the Moate Cross. Turn right down by Lisnavagh House, home of the Bunburys since the 1660s. The house is situated on 600 acres with one third of this given over to beech, ash and oak trees – a beautiful setting. Continue on the road down to the R727, turning left.

Haroldstown Dolmen comes into view at a bend in the road ahead, on the right-hand side and over the bridge on the River Dereen. The dolmen featured on the front cover of Robert Kee's book *A History of Ireland*. It is very similar to the famous Poulnabrone Dolmen in Clare and just as important.

This is a busy, narrow road; take the next right turn to get back onto quieter and safer roads. Turn left at the next crossroads and this will take you to the sleepy village of Clonmore.

Another little village oozing history, Clonmore was a significant monastic site and there are plenty of reminders of its past in the local graveyard which has many old crosses and marked stones and, of course, there are the imposing ruins of Clonmore Castle, which dates to the late thirteenth century.

Continue straight ahead and up a steep hill heading for Hacketstown, where the Barry family farm was. The approach to Hacketstown is dominated by the tabletopped Eagle Hill overlooking the village.

Cross the main road and go down the hill onto the R747, the Kiltegan road. Kiltegan is 6km away just over the border in County Wicklow. Like its

95

parish neighbour Rathvilly, Kiltegan is a past winner of the Irish Tidy Towns (in 1973).

Humewood Castle, an impressive Gothic mansion built by the Hume family who settled here in the fifteenth century, lies just outside the village. It is now owned by American billionaire John C. Malone but is unfortunately strictly off limits.

Continue past the entrance to Humewood and in 2km turn right towards the sleepy village of Rathangan to begin the climb up to the Glen of Imaal. This is a lovely area with terrific views of Keadeen Mountain and Lugnaquilla. The road winds between the two and the hard graft is rewarded with a great downhill as far as the well-signposted McAllister–Dwyer Cottage. The road is rough in places so be careful.

Michael Dwyer was a member of the United Irishmen and fought in the battles of Vinegar Hill, Arklow and Hacketstown. He fought a guerrilla campaign in the region and was forced to move about and use local houses to rest up in. One such house was the one in Dernamuck where he was billeted with a few of his comrades. Unfortunately for them, they were betrayed by an informer and the house was surrounded by British soldiers. After gaining safe passage for the women and children they decided to fight it out against much superior forces. Antrim man Sam McAllister, seeing the inevitable, stood in the doorway to draw the fire of the soldiers and Dwyer managed to escape across the snow-covered mountains.

It struck me that the rebels Kevin Barry and Michael Dwyer are connected, albeit tenuously, by the River Slaney which flows down from Lugnaquilla, beneath the cottage and on through Baltinglass (where there is a statue to McAllister) and to Rathvilly.

A kilometre after leaving the cottage make a left-hand turn and pass by the rear of Coolmoney Army Camp, the training base for many Irish peacekeeping missions around the world. I wouldn't fancy being billeted here during a snowy winter!

Continue on this quiet, narrow road for 4km and then turn right at a T-junction. Turn left at the next T-junction and stay on the road for 3km approximately before turning right and then right again. This will take you to the busy N81 at Tuckmill. Turn left onto the N81 but it is only for 800 metres. Take a side road signposted for Shrughaun along the side of Baltinglass Hill and into the busy market town of Baltinglass.

Turn left in the square and continue past the secondary school, then make a right-hand turn onto a side road that will lead you back to the Moate Cross just outside Rathvilly. Turn right at the cross to return to your starting point.

20. Lap of the Lakes

*Kilcullen – Ballymore Eustace – Valleymount – Ballyknockan
– Lacken – Blessington – Brannockstown – Kilcullen*

Location: Counties Kildare and Wicklow

Distance: 67km

Verdict: Exceptional beauty on fine cycling roads

Duration: 3–3½ hours

Grade: 3

Height Gain: 638 metres

Start/Finish

Kilcullen is just off the M9 (take the R448 exit at Junction 2) and is about 50km south of Dublin.

Parking is at a premium in Kilcullen but you should be able to find spaces in the car park beside the Church.

Cycling through Lacken on the Blessington Lakes circuit

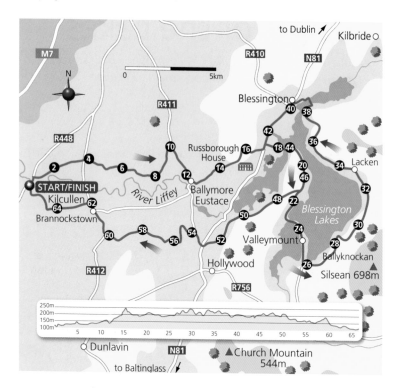

Route Highlights

Kilcullen is horse country and the roads around the town are bordered by pristine stud farms – so different from the wilderness on the east bank of the Blessington Lakes. It's a route of contrast with stunning lake and mountain scenery along the undulating lakeshore road.

Route Description

Kilcullen is a small town located on the River Liffey just 12km south of Naas. It was formerly known as Kilcullen Bridge to distinguish it from Old Kilcullen, which is located a couple of kilometres south where there was an ancient monastic settlement and a hilltop round tower.

Cycle down the main street and over the River Liffey, then head up the steep hill. Pass the Centra store on the left-hand side and make a right-hand turn just at the top of the hill.

This quiet road will take you across towards Ballymore Eustace. After 3km continue straight at Carnalway Cross. St Patrick's Church is beside the crossroads and is an interesting first stop. Built by the La Touche family in 1891 it contains a Harry Clarke stained-glass window.

Continue straight on a good cycling road and keep an eye out for a mysterious and unmarked ancient cross which is by the roadside behind a wooden fence, about 4km past Carnalway Cross. Locals believe it to date from the seventeenth century. It was originally erected in a nearby graveyard as the base of a cross is located there. It is thought the cross was being transported by horse and cart and that it fell off the cart at this point, where it was erected and has since stood.

Shortly after passing the cross there are road signs warning that the road ahead is closed and it is necessary to take a short detour by turning left onto the L6048 followed by a right after 1.5km and following the signs for Ballymore Eustace. The road is closed apparently because of subsidence, which is a pity, as the closed road runs high above the River Liffey. The detour adds about 2km to the journey.

Ballymore Eustace is on the Kildare/Wicklow border and is an attractive village on the Liffey. It is very close to Russborough House, which you will pass on this route.

At the top of town take care to make a left-hand turn onto a quiet road that will bring you around the back of Russborough House. This Palladian mansion is famous for once holding the Beit art collection and was subjected to some well-known robberies, most notably by Rose Dugdale and Martin 'The General' Cahill.

There's a good pull uphill for 3km but it is worth it as the views are great and it means avoiding a longer stretch on the busy N81. Take the first right-hand turn on the descent and follow the wall around Russborough House. Be careful not to miss a left turn, which is not signposted. This narrow road will lead you close to the turnoff for Valleymount and ensures your distance on the N81 is a mere 300 metres.

If you miss the left turn, continue straight to visit Russborough House and then carry on down to the N81 and turn left.

Turn right off the N81 towards Valleymount, which is signposted.

The road passes over the first of three bridges over Blessington Lakes, also known as the Poulaphouca Reservoir. The lakes were formed seventy years ago when a dam and hydroelectric station were constructed at Poulaphouca resulting in the beautiful 20 square kilometres of lakes that we now enjoy. Seventy-six farmhouses and cottages were covered by the lakes when the dam was constructed.

Navigation is simple: follow the road around the main lake in an anticlockwise direction.

After passing through Valleymount, which is located on a spit in the lake, turn left and soon you will roll into Ballyknockan, the granite village. Hard to believe you are only 25km from Dublin city centre in this beautiful wilderness. Ballyknockan retains a sense of remoteness and it could easily be located in Connemara on the west coast of Ireland. The views are sensational from this village, famous for its granite quarries – the stone is evident all around in the farmhouses, cottages and the granite stone walls that enclose small fields down to the lakeshore. If Wicklow is the Garden of Ireland, then Ballyknockan is the rockery in that garden!

Continue around the lake and into Lacken village on a road that constantly rises and falls on a narrow road where it is all too easy be distracted by the breathtaking views. In summertime the road can be busy with day trippers so caution is advised.

If you wish, you can extend this route at Lacken by taking a sharp right-hand turn and continuing up over the hill on a bog road that is poorly surfaced for about 4km. This will add about 10km to the total distance. The bonus is exceptional views of Blessington Lakes and across to Kippure on the other side of the hill. Keep left at the next two junctions and follow the signs back to Blessington.

Take the next left over the bridge, which will take you into Blessington, one of the larger towns in County Wicklow, steeped in history with many fine buildings on the main street.

Continue out of the town on the N81 as far as the turn for Valleymount that you took earlier. Head back towards Valleymount but after 4km take the L8365 towards Tulfarris Hotel.

Turn slightly right after Tulfarris and continue on this road for about 1.5km. The main road veers right but continue straight on to a narrow road for 3km and then turn right and cross over the N81 onto the R411 for 1km. Turn left onto the L5043 and then take a sharp left after another kilometre, followed by a right onto the L6060. Stay on this road for a further 4km, passing through a crossroads.

Turn onto the R412 and admire the beautiful stud farms on both sides of the road, among them Ragusa Stud and Ardenode Stud. It's very pretty horse country. Continue into Brannockstown, turning left at Brannockstown Crossroads onto the R413. This will take you back into Kilcullen and your parking spot, which is on the left-hand side as you enter the town.

21. Dunbrody Trail

New Ross – Ballyhack – Passage East – Cheekpoint – Passage East – Ballyhack – Arthurstown – JFK Memorial Park – Slieve Colitia – New Ross

Location: Counties Wexford and Waterford

Distance: 67km

Duration: 3¾–4¼ hours

Grade: 3

Height Gain: 987 metres

Verdict: Glorious route on scenic roads

Start/Finish

The Dunbrody Famine Ship Experience in New Ross is the spectacular starting point for this route. There are pay-and-display car parks located close by.

Dunbrody Abbey, County Wexford

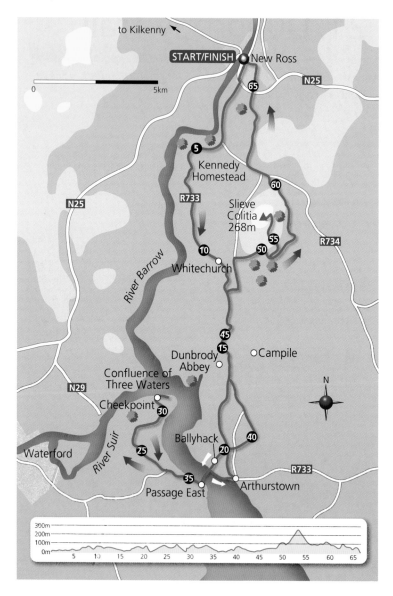

Route Highlights

A route that takes in coastal scenery, a ferry crossing, a mountain with a road to the top with stunning views and some charming seaside villages!

Leaving Ballyhack, County Wexford

Route Description

The *Dunbrody* is an authentic reproduction of an 1840s emigrant vessel and is a wonderful quayside attraction in New Ross. It is a great place to begin this route. Take the N25 ring road out of town and then turn right onto the R733. After 3km take another right onto the L4026 which is signposted for the Kennedy Homestead, the birthplace of John F. Kennedy's great-grandfather Patrick. The land is still farmed by his descendants and there is a wonderful interpretative centre with helpful staff beside the homestead.

It was JFK himself who said, 'Nothing compares to the simple pleasures of a bike ride' and how right he was!

Continue straight through Whitechurch and on to the junction with the R733. Stay straight ahead, following signs for Dunbrody Abbey. Built

103

in 1170 on the instructions of Strongbow, it was one of the first Cistercian monasteries in the country and is an impressive sight from all directions. It can be seen later on from Cheekpoint in Waterford peeking over the inlet across the Barrow.

About a kilometre after the abbey make a right-hand turn uphill for a shortcut to Ballyhack. Turn right turn after 3km and freewheel down into the picturesque village to catch the ferry to Passage East. The ferry crossing is less than five minutes but adds an exotic element to the route. Leave Passage by taking a right-hand turn uphill on the R683 towards Waterford city. After 2km make a right-hand turn onto a quiet road which will bring you over as far as Cheekpoint, the only place you can view the 'Confluence of the Three Waters' – the Barrow, the Nore and the Suir. Great Island Power Station across the estuary unfortunately detracts from the loveliness of the scene.

Retrace your route back to Passage East. There is an alternative off-road section if you don't mind pushing your bike for a distance along a clifftop walking route – you will be rewarded with some stunning scenery if you choose to do so. The walking route can be accessed after Faithlegg national school, turning left down a cul-de-sac and continuing on from there.

On arrival back in Ballyhack, follow the coast road around to Arthurstown – a nice spot for a swim on a summer's day.

Take the first left in Arthurstown and then turn right at the next crossroads onto the L4053. Cross over the R733 and continue to the next crossroads. Away to your left you can see your destination, Slieve Colitia. Turn left and merge with the R733 for 8km. Take the turn for John F. Kennedy Park. The climbing starts immediately and opposite the entrance to the park is a road to the top of Slieve Colitia. This is where you are heading. It's 3km to the top and a darn good pull too! But it is well worth the effort as this is the best vantage point in all of Wexford with amazing views out to the Saltee Islands, down to Hook Head and Dunmore East, and north towards New Ross.

Be careful of the speed bumps on the descent!

On reaching the main road turn left to return to New Ross on back roads. Take a left turn after 2km onto the L8054 which snakes its way across to the R734 and R733. The surface is poor but is OK to cycle on. The main road runs back into New Ross but take the more scenic option: after about 1km make a right-hand turn and enter New Ross on this hilly back road. Cross the ring road and continue straight ahead along Charlton Hill before turning left down Cross Street to return to the quayside and the *Dunbrody*.

All in all, a route to remember.

22. Bagenalstown/ Drumphea Route

Bagenalstown – Ballinkillen – Drumphea – Altamont Gardens – The Fighting Cocks – Bagenalstown

Location: County Carlow

Distance: 69km

Duration: 3–3½ hours

Grade: 3

Height Gain: 652 metres

Verdict: Unspoilt rural route on country roads with great views across County Carlow

Nearing Drumphea, County Carlow

Start/Finish

Bagenalstown, also known as Muine Bheag, is located on the River Barrow just off the M9 south of Carlow. Exit at Junction 6 if coming from Dublin or Junction 7 if coming from Kilkenny. Better still, arrive by train! The starting point is on Station Road adjacent to the beautiful neoclassical railway station, one of Ireland's prettiest. Parking spaces are available on Station Road.

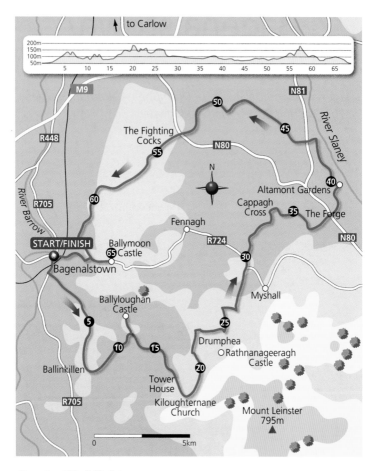

Route Highlights

This route explores the centre of County Carlow and is mainly flat but with two significant hills to add a bit of spice. Between ancient castles, heritage gardens and houses and beautiful rustic scenes, it's a lovely route suitable for all abilities.

Route Description

Bagenalstown is named after its founder, Walter Bagenal, who founded the town in the eighteenth century. His plans were ambitious, to say the least, as he intended it to be a mini Versailles! He began by building the impressive courthouse modelled on the Parthenon of ancient Athens but sadly that is all that remains of his breathtaking plan.

Leaving Drumphea, Carlow's highest village

With the railway station behind you and the McGrath Hall on your left, begin your route by continuing down to the mini-roundabout and taking a left-hand turn onto Kilree Street, heading for Borris. On the way out, you will cross over the railway bridge and see a fine example of traditional Carlow granite fencing on both sides of the approach to the bridge.

Turn left onto the L3001 signposted for Corries Cross.

Continue for about 4km and, as the road begins a gentle climb, make a right-hand turn. This will bring you over to the Church of the Good Shepherd, Lorum. The current church stands on an ancient Christian site. Tradition has it that St Laserian paused at Lorum on his way from Rome, via Wexford as he headed towards Old Leighlin where he founded his religious community.

The road rises and falls on the approach to the sleepy village of Ballinkillen. Turn left at the bottom of the village onto the L3004 heading for Corries Cross just over 2km away and continue straight ahead to the next crossroads.

If you wish to visit Ballyloughan Castle, turn left, otherwise go right. Ballyloughan Castle has one of the finest examples of a twin-towered gatehouse in the country; this, along with the ruins of two other corner towers, is all that remains. Entrance to the site is via two locked gates and it is best to ask for permission at the adjoining farmhouse for access.

Retrace your route back to Corries Cross and continue down the hill to another crossroads. Continue straight ahead in the direction of the signposted Templemoling Cemetery. Along the way you will see a fine example of a tower house, on the right-hand side of the road. A former RIC barracks, it was beautifully renovated some years ago.

Templemoling Cemetery is a very spiritual place with stunning views of the Blackstairs from this ancient graveyard. It is associated with St Moling but only scant remains of a hermitage are visible. There is a large boulder on the site said to contain the footprint of St Finian.

Continue past the cemetery on this narrow boreen and turn left to head towards the highest village in Carlow: Drumphea. Alternatively you could make a small detour to the ancient Kiloughternane Church ruins, which are close by.

It's a steep climb to the hamlet of Drumphea. There are great views in all directions from the village. The church in Drumphea was presented with a chalice in 1397 by the mother of Roger Mortimer, heir apparent to the throne of England. Roger was killed in the Battle of Kellistown that same year and the chalice was given in return for his body.

Leaving Drumphea, continue downhill and take a sharp right back uphill on a small side road. The views are great along this section. Turn left at the next T-junction. The road now runs parallel to the River Burren, which rises close by on Mount Leinster. Take a very sharp left at the next T-junction and continue across to the next crossroads where you turn right, heading towards Myshall. In less than a kilometre take another left onto a side road that runs straight for about 2km. Turn right at the T-junction, followed by a left onto the R724. At the next T-junction a few hundred metres ahead take the side road to the right. The road meanders for some time; then turn left at the T-junction. The terrain is very flat in this part of Carlow and progress is speedy. At the next T-junction go right and after 2km turn right at the signposted Cappagh Crossroads. Just after another kilometre follow the road around to the right and continue on to the next T-junction. Turn left here and up ahead at the Kilbride Crossroads is the Forge Restaurant, which is a great spot to take a break and a little treat.

Suitably revived, cross the N80 and continue on to Altamont Gardens. Widely regarded as one of the premier heritage gardens in the country, it is well worth a visit. It has a stunning array of trees, shrubs and flowering plants plus the wonderful walk through the Bog Garden and Ice Age Glen down to the River Slaney.

On leaving Altamont turn right and continue for 3km to a T-junction. A right-hand turn here will take you down to the Aghade Bridge and fantastic views of the wild River Slaney. However, we turn left on our route and cross over the N81 at the eccentrically named Bang Up Cross.

Shortly after, take a right-hand turn signposted for Sandbrook House and continue on this road for 4km. Take a sharp left followed by a sharp right and then take the next right onto a narrow road.

Continue to a T-junction and take a slight left onto the L3046. Follow the road around the bend and continue on, passing The Fighting Cocks

Altamont Gardens, County Carlow

GAA Grounds to the staggered junction with the N80. Cross over and take a break at the Fighting Cocks pub. (It might be wise to take some refreshments before the steep climb ahead.)

Continue up past the Fighting Cocks and the road begins to rise gently. After about 2km take the side road straight ahead and soon you will be battling one of the severest gradients around to Bradleys Crossroads at the top of the Nurney Plateau.

Continue straight ahead and downhill – with caution as it is very steep – to the next cross and go right. Still heading downhill turn left at the next crossroads, Augha Cross. Augha Church ruins are located just ahead but turn left and continue on this road down to Dunleckney Cross.

Turn left here followed by another left to visit Ballymoon Castle (or continue straight ahead for a slightly shorter route). Turn left onto the R724. Fourteenth-century Ballymoon Castle is up ahead on your left. It is a striking and unusual design comprising a large courtyard surrounded by thick granite walls. Square towers project from three sides with a gatehouse on the fourth.

Turn around to return to Bagenalstown, which is just under 4km away, entering over another railway bridge featuring the unique Carlow granite fencing. Turn left after the bridge to return to the starting point.

23. Paulstown Route

*Paulstown – Castlecomer – Dunmore Cave – Ballyfoyle –
Kilkenny city – Bennettsbridge – Paulstown*

Location: County Kilkenny

Distance: 72km

Duration: 3¼–3¾ hours

Verdict: Quiet roads and some great attractions

Grade: 3

Height Gain: 584 metres

Start/Finish

The route is convenient to the M9 and the starting point is just beside Junction 7, Paulstown. There is space for a couple of cars in front of the graveyard, which is on the Kilkenny side of the village.

Kilkenny Castle

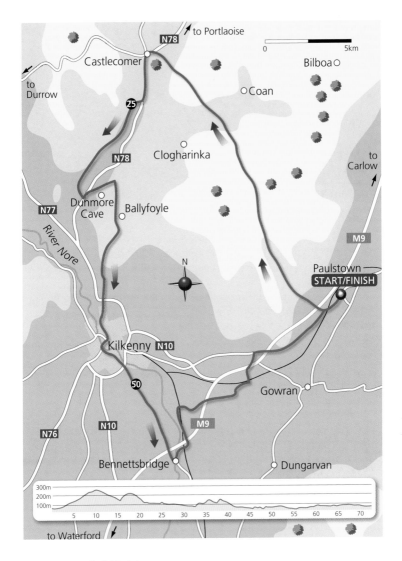

Route Highlights

Kilkenny is full of delights. Taking in a visit to the famed Dunmore Cave and a visit to Kilkenny Castle, the route is a terrific day out for the curious cyclist. The starting point is ideally located close to the motorway services area, handy for a snack before and after the cycle!

The grounds of Kilkenny Castle

Route Description

There is a cycle path all the way from Carlow town to Kilkenny city and this route begins on the cycle path heading towards Kilkenny from Paulstown.

After passing under the railway bridge turn right following the sign for Castlecomer. The road gently rises for 10km onto the Castlecomer plateau. It's a pleasant uphill stretch that causes no strain. Looking back, the views towards Mount Leinster and the Blackstairs are beautiful and on the morning I completed the route the valley was covered in fog with the peaks rising through the white veil – spectacular!

The road uphill is protected from the elements for long stretches with good cover provided by a border of mature ash trees on both sides and there is vey little exposure, even at the top of the hill.

There are great views ahead too as you start the 10km down towards Castlecomer. Turn left at the T-junction with the N78 just outside the town and opposite the fantastic Discovery Park, which has become a major tourist attraction with its coal-mining museum, cafe, craft yard and outdoor adventure areas.

Head up to the top of the square and turn left onto Kilkenny Street, the N78. As this is a busy road make a right-hand turn onto the L1823 in the direction of Conahy/Jenkinstown after about 3km. This is a meandering back road which is part of the North Kilkenny Cycle (NKC) Route. After 7km you meet another signpost for the NKC Route. Ignore this and continue straight ahead until you meet the N78 again.

Turn left back towards Castlecomer and in 500 metres turn right, heading uphill to Dunmore Cave.

The cave is highly recommended for a break. Dunmore Cave has a dark history and the Annals of the Four Masters record a Viking massacre here of 1,000 local people; archaeologists have discovered human remains and signs of Viking activity. There are 500 metres of passages and caverns, and guided tours are available.

Leave the cave and turn right up a kilometre-long section of poorly surfaced road. Turn right at the junction heading in the direction of Ballyfoyle. Just before Ballyfoyle veer right towards Kilkenny city, passing Kilkenny Golf Club and Kilkenny College. At the entrance to the college turn right and then left and a bike path will lead you safely into the city centre.

Use the castle skyline as your marker and make your way in past the James Stephens Barracks and McDonagh Junction Shopping Centre, both on your left. Just across from the barracks is the controversial new bridge under construction.

Kilkenny Castle and grounds are one of the leading tourist attractions in the south-east and it's easy see why. Towering above the River Nore, the twelfth-century seat of the Butlers of Ormond dominates the city. The Castle Gardens are an oasis in this bustling, vibrant city. There is so much to see in and around Kilkenny that it deserves a day to itself.

The bike path continues past the castle and we follow it to exit the city, taking the road for Thomastown/Bennettsbridge. It's a short, flat 7km to Bennettsbridge, a hub for arts and crafts nestling along the Nore.

After crossing the river, make a left-hand turn signposted for Bennettsbridge GAA Club. In the next 3km you will cross the railway line three times, twice at level crossings and once over a bridge. Make a right-hand turn shortly after the second level crossing, followed by another right after 400 metres.

This quiet road will lead you to the Carlow–Kilkenny road, the R722, where you will turn right and pick up the cycle path that will lead you back to Paulstown passing the award-winning Paddy's Country Pub.

All the hard work is done on the first half of this route and the latter half is nice and flat – a good way to finish!

On the Paulstown–Castlecomer road, County Kilkenny

24. Tour of the Blackstairs

Rathanna – Bunclody – Kiltealy – Rathnure – Ballywilliam – Glynn – Ballymurphy – Rathanna

Location: County Carlow

Grade: 4

Distance: 76km

Height Gain: 1,028 metres

Duration: 4–4½ hours

Verdict: No better way to explore the beautiful rural countryside of south Carlow and north-west Wexford than along this route around the Backstairs Mountains. Great views, some nice climbing and almost traffic-free.

Cúl na Sneachta *and beyond, Mount Leinster, County Carlow*

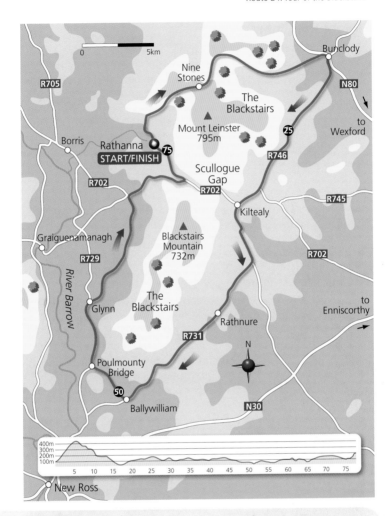

Start/Finish

Rathanna is best accessed via Borris in south County Carlow. Take the signposted road underneath the Borris Viaduct to get there. Borris is situated 30km south of Carlow and about 26km east of Kilkenny. Coming from Carlow, exit the M9 at Junction 6 and continue through Leighlinbridge and Bagenalstown. If coming from Kilkenny, exit the M9 at Junction 7 at Paulstown and continue through Goresbridge to Borris. Rathanna is 8km from Borris. Park beside Osborne's Hostel in Rathanna and head towards the hills!

Route Highlights

The road across the side of Mount Leinster and around the Blackstairs is a dramatic cycle route with spectacular views across Counties Carlow and Wexford. The Blackstairs and south Carlow are becoming quite popular tourist destinations. It's an unspoilt rural landscape devoid of tour buses and the overcrowding of the west coast. The route over the Nine Stones regularly features in the An Post Rás. It's a stunning cycle from all directions, and challenging too.

The Nine Stones is a great viewing point looking over the poetically named *Cúl na Sneachta*, which translates literally from Irish as 'Back of the Snow'. One of the legends concerning the Nine Stones, which stand in a row beside the car park, tells of St Moling travelling hungrily on the road where he met a man with a bag on his back. The saint asked if there was bread in the bag (which there was) but the man replied 'no, stones'. The saint replied, 'if stones, may they be turned into bread and if bread may they be turned into stones!' The stones are still there.

Route Description

Leave the car park and cycle past Osborne's bar, which is on your left. Continue straight ahead and at the next T-junction turn right. After a kilometre you will come to an area known as The Bullring; it's a circular road with four exits. Keep left and take the second exit. It's early in the cycle but you hit a very steep (though short) hill. Turn right at the top, at Tomduff Cross, and in a very short space you cross over a crossroads, Louis's crossroads. You are now heading up the side of Slievebawn on your

Cycling on Mount Leinster, County Carlow

Cycle race on Mount Leinster, County Carlow

left with magnificent Mount Leinster looming above you over your right shoulder. There are fantastic views here across towards the Scullogue Gap which splits the Blackstairs in two and as far as Mount Brandon, over by Graiguenamanagh.

The 4km climb to the Nine Stones from Tomduff is by far the easiest of the three routes up the mountain but is still a good challenge. There are two cattle grids across the road and they don't present much of a challenge ascending but are dangerous coming down.

The Nine Stones is a popular destination for Sunday afternoon spins in the car and is a good place to stop, catch your breath and admire the incredible view across County Carlow. It is possible to cycle to the top of Mount Leinster as there is a road to the TV mast at the summit (795 metres). The road is blocked to cars with a locked gate but access is possible for cyclists. However, the gradient is very severe all the way to the top and is extremely dangerous on the descent.

Our route continues straight ahead and concentration levels need to be high as there is a steep drop on your left as you descend. It's one of the finest cycling roads in the country and a thrilling ride. Care again is needed as there are cattle grids on this stretch.

Turn right at the next T-junction in the Corrabut Gap and the road falls all the way into County Wexford and the beautiful town of Bunclody.

With its lime-tree-adorned central mall and babbling stream, Bunclody is a town with character and charm. It's a nice place to stop for a cuppa before heading out towards Rathnure and around the Blackstairs range.

Take the third exit at the mini-roundabout at the end of the square heading for New Ross on the R746. The road skirts the hills and there are no difficulties in speeding towards Kiltealy 12km away. Turn right onto the R702 just outside Kiltealy and this will lead you into the village.

It's situated on the Wexford side of the Scullogue Gap and the route can be shortened if desired by turning right in Kiltealy and taking a shortcut through the hills.

Staying on course, continue onto the R730 for 4km, then veer right onto the R731 for Rathnure, which is 4km away. Rathnure is famed for its hurling sons – the Rackards, Englishs and Quigleys.

Continue for about 8km to reach Ballywilliam, the southernmost point on this loop.

Turn right opposite the supermarket onto a narrow tree-lined road that takes you down to Poulmounty Bridge, the most southerly tip of County Carlow. The canopy above the road and the rushing waters make for a memorable stretch as the route turns back north and towards the starting point.

Turn right at Poulmounty Bridge and continue to Glynn. Just after Glynn, make a right-hand turn onto a narrow road for about 3km until you meet the L3007. Turn right and continue on this road all the way to Ballymurphy. The road on this side of the Blackstairs is much more interesting and undulating with fine views in all directions.

At Ballymurphy turn right at the T-junction onto the R702 and continue into the Scullogue Gap. Knockroe looms ahead. There is a wonderful example of rock art on the hill to your right at Rathgeran. Ask for directions as it is impossible to find without local knowlege. After 4km approximately take a very sharp left onto a minor road which will lead you back to the village of Rathanna and your finish point 4km away.

25. Inistioge Route

Inistioge – Kilfane – Stoneyford – Kells – Kilree –
Hugginstown – Ballyhale – Tullogher – Inistioge

Location: County Kilkenny

Distance: 80km

Duration: 4½–5 hours

Verdict: Plenty of climbing and some amazing sights

Grade: 5

Height Gain: 1,203 metres

Start/Finish

Inistioge is the starting point for this epic route. Exit the M9 at Junction 9, Kilkenny South, and continue through Bennetsbridge and Thomastown. Park in the village. Leave Inistioge by crossing the Nore Bridge and taking an immediate left.

Looking down into Inistioge on the return leg

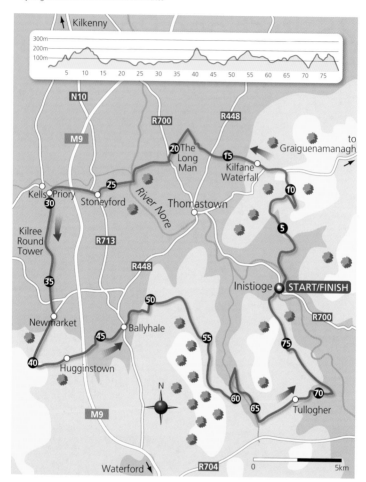

Route Highlights

This challenging but rewarding route takes in a surprising amount of hills as it goes along some beautiful scenic routes that are seldom travelled. Starting in one of the most visited places in the south-east, Inistioge on the banks of the River Nore, this cycle has many fascinating points of interest – it's an area rich in heritage sites, wonderful scenery and many native woodland trees along the way.

Route Description

Inistioge has long been a Mecca for visiting fishermen, nature enthusiasts and artists. This historic village, with its tree-lined square, has a relaxed and welcoming feel and is worth an extended stay if possible.

Crossing the bridge over the River Nore at Inistioge, County Kilkenny

Follow the signs for the East Kilkenny Cycle (EKC) route over the bridge and then left along a road running parallel to the Nore on its east bank. Across the river is surely one of the nicest settings for any GAA pitch in the country!

The EKC is a pretty route but our paths diverge at the second junction just 2km up the road, where we go right, and we start rising in the direction of Coppanagh Hill. Take care over the next few kilometres at the various junctions as the roads are not signposted and caution is needed. In another 2km continue straight ahead and do not take the right-hand turn. The road continues to rise gradually – nothing too severe – and there are wonderful views back towards Inistioge and across the hills. Turn right at the next T-junction. The road begins to follow the contours of Coppanagh Hill and eventually meets the L4203 at the top of the climb. Turn left heading down towards Thomastown and, after 1km, at a bend on this main road, go straight onto a minor road, which will take you to pretty Kilfane Glen and Waterfall (Heritage Gardens). The descent is rapid and at the bottom of the hill be sure to call in to the thirteenth-century Kilfane Church to see The Long Man! This effigy of a Norman knight in full armour stands 2 metres tall inside the church ruins. Getting back on the road, make a right-hand turn onto the R448 and a quick left beside the Long Man Pub, heading towards Stoneyford.

Turn left at the next crossroads, again merging onto the EKC and following it back in the direction of Thomastown. Turn left onto the R700 followed by a right, heading for Stoneyford 5km distant. The road skirts the Mount Juliet Golf Resort and crosses over the River Nore en route.

Turn right and head up the main street of Stoneyford to the top of the town and then left onto the L1023 for the village of Kells. Just before the village is the impressive Kells Priory. This Augustinian priory is an important national monument. The tower houses along the walls enclosing the 3 acres of the priory give it the look of a fortress rather than a monastic foundation. Worth stopping to explore!

Our route doesn't continue into the village but it is an option as a nice stopping-off point on the banks of the King's River. Instead we cross the road from the priory and head 3km due south which takes us to Kilree Round Tower. This has a highly atmospheric, hauntingly beautiful setting in a wooded graveyard on top of a hill with great views of the surrounding countryside. On the far side of the round tower is a ninth-century sandstone high cross. A word of caution: signs on the gate as you cross to the round tower warn to beware of the bull!

Continue south past the round tower and enjoy the nice, flat roads, as that will change soon! In 4km cross over the R699 and then turn right onto the R701 for a short distance before taking a right turn towards the signposted Aghaviller church ruins and round tower, one of five round towers in the county. The road rises sharply from here through a wooded area and the gradient is steep and challenging.

Heading towards Coppanagh Hill after leaving Inisitioge, County Kilkenny

Turn left at the top and continue along this road through three crossroads heading into Hugginstown. Turn right in the village and then immediately left onto the L8255. After 2km turn left at the T-junction with the L8256 followed by a right turn after 500 metres onto a narrow road that will bring you into Ballyhale. This town is famous for its magnificent hurlers, none more renowned than Henry Shefflin, holder of a record ten All-Ireland Senior Hurling medals.

Turn left in the village, followed by a right, and the road begins to rise gradually again. Turn left onto the L8253 followed by an immediate right onto the L8252. After passing through a level crossing, take the next left at a T-junction. Take a sharp right a kilometre later and the next right in the direction of Chapel Hill until you meet a T-junction after another 3km. Turn right. (This section features as part of our Ollie Walsh route – see route 28.)

Just after 3km further, take a very narrow road down to the bottom of the valley and the Arrigle River. This is a poor section of road and can be avoided if you desire by continuing straight and taking the next left. At the bottom of the hill turn left and cross over the Arrigle River then take a sharp right turn.

Soon after this there is a shorter way back to Inistioge by heading uphill at T-junction. We continue straight past this turn and in 3km turn left at a crossroads heading for Tullogher. Take the right fork in Tullogher and head downhill for 3km to a T-junction at the bottom. Take a sharp left and gradually climb above the beautiful Nore Valley, which is on your right-hand side. There are some great views here of the valley with its lovely native woodlands. The road passes by Woodstock Gardens on your return to Inistioge.

Be careful on your descent into the village as the road is extremely steep. There is a magnificent view of the River Nore and the bridge below to finish off this momentous cycle route.

26. North Kilkenny Cycle Route

*Castlecomer – Ballyragget – Freshford – Tullaroan –
Ballycallan – Three Castles – Jenkinstown – Castlecomer*

Location: County Kilkenny

Distance: 81km

Duration: 4–4½ hours

Grade: 4

Height Gain: 855 metres

Verdict: Well-marked trail on quiet, well-surfaced roads

Start/Finish

Castlecomer in north Kilkenny is the start and finish point for this marked
Kilkenny trail. It is 31km from Junction 8, Kilkenny North, on the M9. Take
the outer ring road around the city and follow the N77 and then the N78.
Parking is available along the square.

Early climb out of Castlecomer, County Kilkenny

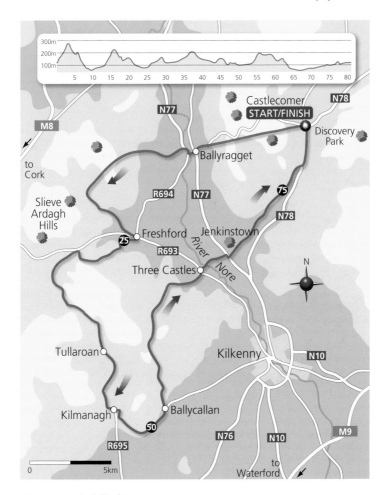

Route Highlights

There are four marked cycle routes in County Kilkenny and this is by far the longest. It is well marked and easy to navigate as a result. The route winds its way through some beautiful countryside and charming villages with a sprinkling of hills in the first half of the loop.

   i found this to be a really pleasant cycle route, with good surfaces, for the most part, on quiet roads.

Route Description

The village of Castlecomer was once the centre of a great coal-mining industry across the Castlecomer plateau. It's still a busy market town and great work has gone into promotion of tourism in the area with Castlecomer Discovery Park now a major attraction and worth a visit.

From the square, cycle uphill and be prepared for an early shock to the system: the first 3km are quite strenuous as you climb along a straight road with magnificent views back to Castlecomer and northwards over your right shoulder.

It's a quiet back road and runs straight virtually all the way to Bally-ragget. After that initial lung-bursting start there is a welcome descent into the village. Ballyragget is situated on a wide, open plain surrounded by pretty hillsides and it is an attractive setting.

The global food giant Glanbia is a mainstay of the economy of the region. Born out of amalgamations of small cooperatives, Avonmore Creamery and Waterford Co-Op Society, in the 1960s, Avonmore constructed what was then the largest multipurpose dairy plant in Europe in Ballyragget. The company now employs 6,000 people across the globe.

The route heads out of town in the direction of the Glanbia Plant which dominates the skyline. Do not follow the road signs for Freshford, which is a dangerous road for cycling, but continue to follow the North Kilkenny Cycle (NKC) route signs. These will bring you there along a nice, quiet back road through Lisdowney with a gentle rise before falling towards Foyle Bridge. The Durrow Cycle route intersects with this route along this section.

Foyle Bridge crosses a pretty little stream where you take the left-hand turn. It's easy cycling into Freshford, a charming village with an expansive tree-lined green. The Irish conker championships take place here each year! The green is a nice place to take a short break.

Leave the green by turning right at the corner you entered from. The road is narrow and bumpy in places as far as Delaney's pub 6km away. Turn left at Delaney's on the minor road and continue straight ahead and in another 3km cycle through a crossroads and pass the Valley Inn/Comerfords and then turn left. It is all signposted to here but take care at the next T-junction as there is a signpost missing for the North Kilkenny Cycle Route. Take the left-hand turn and continue on this road to the next T-junction, which again is not signposted. There is a church and graveyard on the left of the Killahy Crossroads. Turn left here.

Signposting resumes after this and there are no more difficulties in route finding. Follow the signs into the village of Tullaroan. The Slieveardagh Hills are away to the right; there are wonderful views on all sides. Brod Tullaroan, which incorporates the Lory Meagher Heritage Centre, is located in a restored seventeenth-century thatched mansion. It opens during the tourist season and contains a large amount of GAA memorabilia.

With directional signs in place the route is simple to navigate: follow the signs towards Kilmanagh and Ballycallan. About 3km outside

The green at Freshford, County Kilkenny

Kilmanagh is Ballykeeffe Amphitheatre, an outdoor arts venue in an old quarry.

Shortly after the amphitheatre the R697 turns sharp left; continue on it until the left turn for Three Castles and Jenkinstown. The route begins to climb again but is not too difficult. It doubles back in a northerly direction. The road surfaces are really good for most of this route and this particular stretch of the route is great cycling. It is impossible to go astray as the excellent signage guides you to Three Castles and the junction with the R693. Turn left here, then right soon afterwards, crossing over the River Nore and onto the N77. Turn right and then left, passing the attractive Conahy Shamrocks GAA grounds and then by Jenkinstown Park. This is a lovely resting point with picnic areas and lovely walking trails and a deer park.

Continue straight past. The quiet road winds its way for the final 10km or so into Castlecomer.

27. The Three Sisters Tour

Piltown – Mooncoin – Thatched Villages – Granagh Castle – Kilmacow – Slieverue – Glenmore – Mullinavat – Templeorum – Piltown

Location: County Kilkenny   **Grade:** 5

Distance: 88km   **Height Gain:** 1,004m

Duration: 4–4½ hours

Verdict: A strenuous but rewarding route through south Kilkenny with plenty of climbing and a visit to some unique thatched villages.

Start/Finish

Exit the M9 at Junction 12 at Waterford. Follow the N24 through Mooncoin and into Piltown. Park at the Old Creamery Enterprise centre in the centre of Piltown village in south Kilkenny.

The Rivers Barrow and Nore heading to meet the River Suir near Slieverue, County Kilkenny

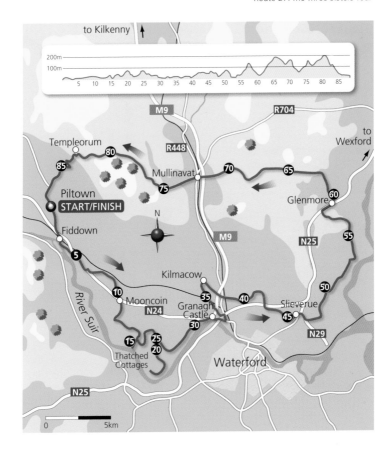

Route Highlights

The name of this route commemorates the mythical Three Sisters – the Barrow, the Nore and the Suir, three great rivers steeped in Irish folklore and history. Used for military purpose and then trade, the rivers are now a source of recreation for visitors to the region. Starting in deepest south Kilkenny close to the banks of the Suir, this route soon winds its way through a hidden enclave, situated in a curve of the Suir, the thatched villages of south Kilkenny. It's such a unique area that it even has its own dialect of English.

The Three Sisters are so called because the three rivers join together to flow into the sea at Waterford. The Barrow and The Nore meet up first and are joined by the Suir at the 'Confluence of the Three Waters'.

The rivers provide pleasant sights for cycling alongside and the route is peppered with some good climbing and great cycling roads.

Route Description

Exit the car park and turn left to cycle up onto the main road and head out of town in the direction of Mooncoin.

Continue down to the bridge at Fiddown over the Suir; there is an important island nature reserve in the middle of the river. The Bridge House was once a tollhouse collecting tolls from travellers, but you need not worry!

Retreat to the road you came on and turn right; soon you will join the busy N24 for about 2km. Turn left off the main road and head across country into Mooncoin. You have the option of going more directly there via the N24 but who wants to be on the busy hard shoulder?

The L717 will take you into and out of the village immortalised in the song 'The Rose of Mooncoin', the official anthem of County Kilkenny.

The road takes you down into a curve in the River Suir where the thatched villages of south Kilkenny are located in the townlands of Licketstown, Glengrant, Moonveen, Luffany and Carrigeen. I was intrigued when I read about the thatched villages recently in John Keane's *Hidden Kilkenny* and cycling through them is like a journey back in time. It really is unspoiled, a parallel universe where time has stood still. Remarkably, John Keane mentions that the area even has a dialect that exists nowhere else and a form of English going back to Elizabethan times.

The area is criss-crossed with many minor roads and a good sense of direction is helpful to avoid having to retrace your steps.

After 1km from crossing the N24, turn left and take the next right. The roads are narrow and quiet. Keep right at the next T-junction (Old Luffany) and follow the road down to the River Suir. The river is very wide here and there are extensive reeds on the riverbank. Retrace your path to the junction and head right again. The road here can be messy – a large dairy herd had turned the road green when I passed by! Turn left at the next T-junction (New Luffany) and take the next two right turns to enter the tiny village of Carrigeen. Take the road up the hill past the church and follow it to the end to see some great examples of thatched houses; however, you must come back into the village to pick up the route again.

Take a sharp right and follow the road for the next 5km or so with lovely views across the Suir into County Waterford. The road joins the N24 again here but only for a short distance, until Granagh Castle and the modern motorway bridge over the Suir come into view.

Granagh Castle is an impressive ruin (legend has it that tunnels leading from it pass under the Suir to the far side in Waterford, which were used to keep the inhabitants stocked with supplies during sieges) with a nice thatched cafe just across the road.

After visiting the castle stay right, going under the M9, before making a left turn and then following the signs for Kilmacow. As you come into the

The thatched villages of County Kilkenny

village make a right turn, followed by a sharp right onto the L3405 heading for Slieverue.

The road passes over the motorway, then crosses the old R448 and brings you into Slieverue. Cycle to the roundabout at the edge of the village and turn right onto the N29 for a short distance. Take the first left-hand turn off it and continue straight ahead for 1.2km. Turn left at the T-junction. There are a few rises and falls but nothing too dramatic and soon the Barrow, which has been joined by the Nore further north, comes into view. It's worth stopping at any vantage point you can to appreciate the views across the river into Wexford and back south towards the confluence. It's a rare sight, off the beaten track.

The road eventually sweeps away from the river and begins to climb, bringing you eventually onto the very busy New Ross–Waterford road, which you must join by turning right. Take care at this dangerous junction. After 1km turn left and take a deserved break in the village of Glenmore. The convenience store is a welcome sight.

Continue down the hill past the Garda station on the left, then make a left-hand turn onto the L3424 which will take you climbing for about 6km but nothing too strenuous. And you have the pleasure of a swift downhill into Mullinavat to look forward too.

Cross the main street in Mullinavat and continue straight ahead for 3km approximately and then take the right fork in the road. It's a lovely hillside road that winds its way around to Templeorum. There is a real treat after leaving the village with a number of switchbacks as you descend in the direction of Piltown. It's a nice way to finish the route and brings you back to base, passing by Kildalton Agricultural College.

28. Ollie Walsh Way

Thomastown – Mullinavat – Owning – Windgap – Killamery – Callan – Newmarket – Thomastown

Location: County Kilkenny

Grade: 5

Distance: 90km

Height Gain: 974 metres

Duration: 4½–5 hours

Verdict: Great hills through remote parts of Kilkenny, featuring high crosses, a dolmen and a passage tomb

Poulanassy Waterfall, Mooncoin, County Kilkenny

Start/Finish

Thomastown is easily accessed from the M9. Exit at Junction 9, Kilkenny South, and continue through Bennetsbridge to Thomastown. Park beside the statue of legendary Kilkenny hurling goalkeeper Ollie Walsh, just over the bridge on the old Waterford road.

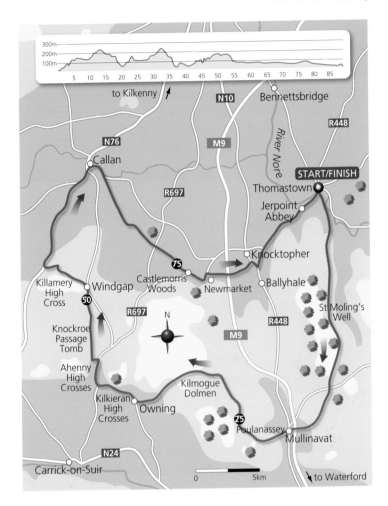

Route Highlights

The surprising aspect of this clockwise route is the amount of climbing involved. Kilkenny may not have any mountains but it certainly contains plenty of wonderful hills full of fascinating sights. It is a very rural county with only two towns with a population greater than 2,000 (Thomastown and Callan) apart from the city. It's an area of natural and stunning beauty, a true rural retreat. Along this route are many places of interest to visit and break the journey.

St Moling's Well, Mullenakill, County Kilkenny

Route Description

With the statue of Ollie Walsh on your left shoulder leave picturesque Thomastown and take an immediate left, following the signs for St Moling's Well 11km distant. It's a beautiful start to the route, cycling under great beech trees that line the road out of the village with glimpses of the River Nore visible through breaks in the tree cover.

It's a gentle uphill pull, following the signs for the well. The views are breathtaking as you gain height. The well is worth a visit – and a welcome break after the early climb.

Continue straight ahead with the magnificent views across the valley and the River Arrigle, still climbing for another 3km until you eventually crest the hill and speed down into Mullinavat. Cross over the main street and the road rises again before you.

Follow the signs for the South Leinster Way, which take you onto the L323 straight ahead.

Just 2km out of the village, on your right, there is an amazing swimming spot on the Poulanassy River, beside a fabulous waterfall which is very popular with locals. It is not signposted and it's easy to miss the laneway down but cars parked on the side of the road usually mark the entrance point. Even if you are not tempted to swim, it is worth looking at.

The climb steepens just after here and, after a sharp bend in the road, you take the next right. The roads are narrow and there are few directional signs.

At a fork in the road after 2km, go right and stay on the road until a sign to the left for Kilmogue Dolmen, aka *Leac an Scail* – a spectacular example of a portal dolmen, and the tallest in Ireland.

It is slightly off the road and if you visit, turn left on your return to the road. After about 4km, turn right onto a larger road and then left. This will bring you downhill into the village of Owning.

Leac an Scail Dolmen, Irelands's tallest portal Dolmen, County Kilkenny

Turn right onto the R698 and catch a glimpse of Slievenamon (*Sliabh na mBan*) in the distance – the Tipperary mountain celebrated in the famous song of the same name.

Over the next few stretches of the route is a group of impressive high crosses – the Ossory group, the first three crosses of which are at Kilkieran just beneath the road on your left.

Just past Kilkieran continue straight at the crossroads onto the R697.

After 2km turn left onto a bridge that crosses over the River Lingaun and continue to the quaint village of Ahenny. More high crosses are signposted to your left. After visiting the crosses retrace your route and continue straight ahead onto the narrow L2412.

After 2km there is a left turn that looks like an entrance to a farmyard that takes you to the significant and unheralded Knockroe Passage Tomb, which is aligned with the winter solstice. It is the most important prehistoric site in Kilkenny. It predates the pyramids, Newgrange and Stonehenge – and it's not even signposted! It is well known to modern-day druids who recognise its significance and I highly recommend a visit.

Back on the route continue uphill through the village of Windgap until the L103 and go left. This takes you to Killamery High Cross before continuing down to the N76. Turn right and follow the road into Callan. It's a good, wide road though it can be busy.

Leave Callan on the R699 in the direction of Knocktopher. The R699 takes a left turn just outside Callan but go straight ahead onto a quiet side road just at a bend on the R699. Continue for 10km to reach Castlemorris Wood.

Continue into Newmarket and turn right onto the L4211, a very minor road.

Turn right at the junction with the R713 heading for Ballyhale followed by a left onto the R448 which will take you back to Thomastown via Jerpoint Abbey. Nearby in Jerpoint Park the remains of St Nicholas of Myra, the original Santa Claus, are reputedly buried.

It's only a short skip back into Thomastown to your parking spot beside Ollie Walsh!

29. Slieve Blooms – The Three Peaks Challenge

Rosenallis – Glenbarrow – Clonaslee – Kinnitty – Glendine –

Camross – Ballyfin – Rosenallis

Location: Counties Laois and Offaly

Distance: 92km

Duration: 5–5½ hours

Grade: 5

Height Gain: 1,363 metres

Verdict: Fantastic climbing and wonderful scenery

Crossing the Slieve Bloom Mountains, County Laois

Start/Finish

Rosenallis is situated 15km north-west of Portlaoise. Exit the M7 at any one of Junctions 16, 17 or 18 into Portlaoise. Follow the N80 to Mountmellick and from there the R422 will take you to Rosenallis. There is parking available on the R422 just around the bend after the Catholic church.

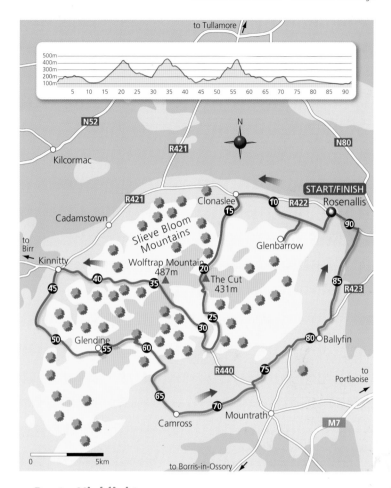

Route Highlights

The Slieve Bloom Mountains have everything: great climbs, great descents, mountains, valleys, pretty villages, waterfalls, forests and blanket bogs. This route is simply amazing!

Route Description

Accessible from all parts of Ireland, the Slieve Bloom Mountains are conveniently located along the Laois/Offaly border, yet are totally underexplored. They are a place of peace, solitude and birdsong.

Turn right out of the car park in the Quaker village of Rosenallis and take the road signposted for Glenbarrow. After you leave the village, in

Descending in the Slieve Bloom Mountains, heading towards Kinnitty

the high banks along the roadside is a profusion of ferns and gorse. The road is narrow and quiet. Turn right after 1.5km and then left in another 1.5km. This will bring you to the source of Ireland's second-longest river, the Barrow. The road in from this point is poor and needs resurfacing but it is only a short distance in and is worth the effort.

There is a small car park before entering the forest walk that takes you to the waterfall at Glenbarrow; you can bring your bike in and cycle or walk most of the way to the falls. The path is covered in a dense layer of pine needles and I recommend locking your bike to one of the trees and proceeding the short distance on foot because it becomes rocky.

This is one of the most scenic areas in the Slieve Blooms with its waterfall and steep valley. Give yourself an hour to enjoy this hidden gem.

Resume your route by cycling back out to the T-junction, where you turn left. It's an easy 10km to the edge of Clonaslee. Our route will take in three peaks – The Cut, The Wolftrap and Glendine.

Take a left-hand turn just as you approach Clonaslee and this road will lead all the way to the top at the place called The Cut. There are great views on the way up and the gradient is kind to the top, which is 439 metres high. It is said that on a clear day you can see as far as Armagh from here.

Sitka spruce and lodgepole pine dominate most of the coniferous woodlands of the Slieve Blooms, the largest cover of forestry in Ireland. Broadleaf species like birch and willow grow profusely along the valley floors; and oak, alder, rowan and holly are also common. The trees in places form a wonderful canopy over the roads, giving great cover and making the route all the more enchanting.

The descent down from The Cut is on a great surface and there are a number of hairpin bends to enjoy.

When you finally reach a T-junction, Burke's Cross, turn right in the direction of Kinnitty, County Offaly. The views are spectacular and as you reach the uplands the landscape changes to extensive blanket bog. This is considered to be one of the best and least disturbed areas of blanket bog in the country and is a Special Area of Conservation. The highest point is 456 metres.

The descent into Kinnitty is spectacular with a fabulous surface and exhilarating switchbacks. This attractive village is a good stopping-off point and home to Kinnitty Castle. There is a tenth-century high cross in the grounds of the castle.

Turn left in Kinnitty and continue on a level road for about 5km before turning left to head back into the hills: follow signs for Glendine. Slowly but surely the road begins to rise from pretty farmland into forestry. This is a very remote stretch and quite isolated. It's a long climb which peaks at 449 metres followed by a very steep descent with gradients of 10% in places.

Follow the signs for Camross, another pretty Slieve Bloom village. At the crossroads just outside the village continue straight onto the L1036. Stay on this road for 7km until it meets the R440. Turn left, then shortly afterwards turn right onto another minor road, the L1075, heading for Ballyfin.

This road joins with the R423. Keep straight and cycle past Ballyfin Demesne, an exclusive luxury hotel, voted the top hotel in the world by readers of *Condé Nast Traveller* in 2016 – hard to imagine it was formerly a Patrician Brothers boarding school! The road curves around the boundary of the demesne and, when it straightens out, turn left onto the L2095. In 7km turn left onto the R422, which will bring you back to the car park 2km away.

Glendine, Slieve Bloom Mountains, County Laois

30. Follow Me Up to Carlow

Carlow – Milford – Leighlinbridge – Bagenalstown –
Goresbridge – Graiguenamanagh – St Mullins – Clashganny –
Borris – Fenagh – Newtown – Nurney – Tinryland – Carlow

Location: County Carlow

Distance: 103km

Duration: 4½–5½ hours

Grade: 5

Height Gain: 704 metres

Verdict: This route combines the very best of the Barrow Way with some outstanding river and mountain views in Carlow and some nice climbing, too.

Cycling the Barrow Way, near St Mullins, County Carlow

Start/Finish

Carlow is 100km south-west of Dublin. Take exit 4 off the M9 and follow the R448 to the second roundabout. Turn left onto the N80 (O'Brien Road). Continue to the second roundabout and take the second exit, continuing straight ahead. After 500 metres, turn right and park in the public car park beside Askea Church.

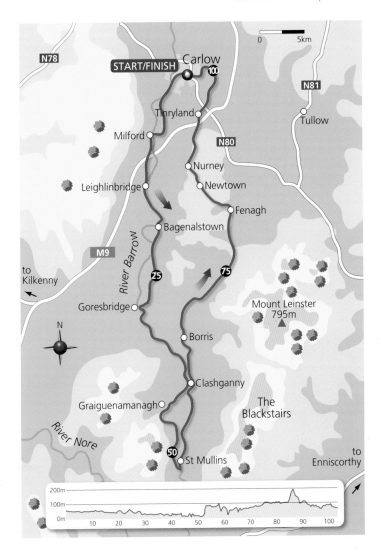

Route Highlights

The finest off-road cycle route in the country is along the Barrow Way (which recently made the shortlist of the top five best days out in Ireland, a competition organised by *The Irish Times* and Discover Ireland.) This route dips in and out of the Barrow Way taking in the most bike-friendly and scenic sections. It's possible to complete the Carlow–St Mullins section on the Barrow Way in its entirety or to parallel it on the road.

Route Description

The Barrow Way is suitable for touring bikes, mountain bikes and hybrid bikes. Road cyclists can omit the off-road sections and follow the route by road.

Turn right onto the O'Brien Road from your parking space at Askea Church. Continue through the roundabout using the bike lane to bring you towards Éire Óg GAA Club. Take the last exit on the roundabout and continue under the railway bridge. Follow the directional signs for Kilkenny. A bike path links Carlow with Kilkenny: follow it out of town past IT Carlow. After 5km turn right at a staggered junction, which takes you down to the River Barrow at Milford. This is a very picturesque setting between the weir and the bridge.

Pass over the two beautiful bridges and turn left at the T-junction. The road will bring you into historic Leighlinbridge 5km distant. When you meet the R448, cross over this busy road and pass down by the award-winning Arboretum Home and Garden Heaven on your left.

Leighlinbridge is a pretty, historic village worth exploring and is a good place to stop for a break. The Valerian Bridge over the Barrow is reputedly one of the oldest functioning bridges in Europe. Beside the bridge is the Black Castle, one of the earliest Norman castles in the country.

Located nearby is Dinn Rí, once the home of the Kings of Leinster. Among the famous sons of Leighlinbridge are the scientist John Tyndall, Captain Myles Kehoe who died at the Battle of the Little Bighorn, Cardinal Patrick Moran, Archbishop of Sydney; it is also the ancestral home of the family of Brian Mulroney, former prime minister of Canada. A memorial garden beside the river has information plaques on these illustrious names.

Go over the bridge and turn onto the Barrow Way. The route continues off-road to Bagenalstown. (If staying on the road, continue straight ahead and take the road uphill, signposted for Bagenalstown.)

This is a nice, short stretch of about 5km along the Barrow Way and, passing Rathellin Lock, will take you into Bagenalstown. There is an outdoor pool on the way for those who fancy a quick dip. Continue along the quay as it follows the bend in the river and make a left-hand turn on Hotel Street, onto High Street.

Continue to Church Street, turn left at the junction and turn right at the mini-roundabout onto the Borris Road. Stay on this road until the turn for Goresbridge after 4km. (If you want to stay on the road, continue straight all the way to Borris). On arrival at Goresbridge, turn on the Barrow Way before crossing over the bridge.

The River Barrow is the second-longest river in Ireland, at 192km. It flows through some of the most scenic countryside in the south-east and forms the Carlow/Kilkenny county boundary.

Clashganny viewing point near Borris, County Carlow

The Barrow Valley south of Goresbridge is unspoilt and yet to become a mainstream tourist destination. Forests of native broadleaf trees and green conifer climbing up the steep slopes of the valley while pleasure boats navigate the many locks of this navigable waterway. To add to its appeal the riverside towns and villages are among the best-kept secrets of the region, providing quality food and accommodation. There are plans to develop a Blueway, an unbound hard surface more suitable to cycling, though it is controversial as the grassy path is much loved by walkers, hikers and fishermen.

It's impossible to go astray as you follow the river south; enjoy its beauty as you following this unique off-road trail to Graiguenamanagh, a busy village worthy of a stop. The sight of all the boats moored along both sides of the river, which is quite wide here, gives a real holiday atmosphere to Graigue. The thirteenth-century Duiske Abbey is a national monument and worth a visit.

Moving on, the river scenery becomes even more beautiful as the deep and dark Barrow winds its way south to the sea and the grassy path is well worn, for it is a very popular walking route.

The small village of St Mullins in south Carlow is a real hidden gem. This was a major ecclesiastical site founded by St Moling. There is a small museum on the site with lots of interesting artefacts. The graveyard is worth a visit, with the ruins of five churches, a round tower and high cross. It's a popular stopping-off point on the river for boats and day visitors.

Leave St Mullins on the Graiguenamanagh road (L3008) – be ready for a short heavy pull uphill past Teampall na Bó. A small church was built here to commemorate St Moling who freed the people of Leinster from the Borumean Tribute – an annual payment to the High King of Ireland of 5,000 cows, 5,000 sheep, 5,000 hogs, 5,000 cloaks, 5,000 bronze vessels and 5,000 ounces of silver! The site was also reputedly used to bury unbaptised babies and there is an annual mass held here for these children on the feast of St Moling, 17 June. It is an evocative setting.

When you arrive at the entrance to Carrigleade Golf Course, veer right onto an even smaller road. There are great views across to the Blackstairs all the way to Borris. Follow the signs for Borris at the next two junctions.

A short while after, you will reach the viewing point above Clashganny Lock. A break in the treeline opens up a fabulous panorama. This is the most photographed scene in County Carlow and on a fine day, with the lock and the Barrow down below set against the patchwork of green fields stretching towards Borris House, it really is a sight to behold.

A nice downhill follows as you speed towards the quaintest town in Carlow, Borris, 5km away. Just before the town, the Borris Viaduct comes into view on your right-hand side. Borris is popular with weekend visitors from all over the country and has some lovely old-style pubs.

Turn right in the centre of the village onto the L3003 heading for Fenagh 15km away.

Continue into Fenagh, past beautiful stone cottages on your right-hand side and go straight ahead at the mini-roundabout. Take the next left about 1km out of the village for the sister village of Newtown. At Newtown church take another right, heading up hill. Turn right at the next T-junction and continue to the highest point on the Nurney plateau in the centre of County Carlow. The hard work is rewarded with stunning views across towards the Killeshin Hills to the west, the Wicklow Mountains to the east and back towards Mount Leinster to the south.

It's a welcome descent into the tiny village of Nurney. Continue straight ahead through Tinryland until the junction with the N80, the Carlow–Wexford road. Cross over the staggered junction. Turn right downhill at the next T-junction then left and cross over the River Burrin. At the next T-junction with the R725 swing right and stay on the road past the Kernanstown housing estate, then turn left.

The road brings you through Bennekerry village. At the next crossroads, turn left in the direction of Carlow town. After 1km you will see a parking bay on your left and the entrance to the Browneshill Dolmen. This dolmen has the largest capstone of any in Europe.

Continue straight ahead into Carlow, turning left at the traffic lights onto the link road. Take the next right onto the Browneshill Road and this will bring you back to your parking spot at Askea Church.